Susan Frutkin

WITHDRAWN

AIMÉ CÉSAIRE
BLACK BETWEEN WORLDS

MONOGRAPHS IN INTERNATIONAL AFFAIRS

CENTER FOR ADVANCED INTERNATIONAL STUDIES
UNIVERSITY OF MIAMI
1973

Susan Frutkin received her undergraduate degree in history from Smith College. During two years in Switzerland, she studied at the University of Geneva's prestigious Institut des Hautes Etudes Internationales and simultaneously became fluent in French. Pursuing her specialty in International Relations, Mrs. Frutkin received her M.A. from the Center for Advanced International Studies, University of Miami, where she wrote the prize-winning thesis that inspired this book. Mrs. Frutkin, who was a free-lance writer for several years, is now a Researcher/Editor with Booz, Allen Applied Research in Washington, D.C.

Cover design by
Arnold W. Frutkin

To A.W.F.
with all my love

"Césaire had spoken for those who could not speak and those who could not speak thronged around the table to shake his hand, and kiss him . . . What made him so attractive now was the fact that he, without having ceased to be one of them, yet seemed to move with the European authority. He had penetrated into the heart of the great wilderness which was Europe and stolen the sacred fire. And this, which was the promise of their freedom, was also the assurance of his power."

James Baldwin, from an account of the 1956
International Conference of Black Writers
and Artists in *Nobody Knows My Name*

Table of Contents

FOREWORD

The Center for Advanced International Studies of the University of Miami takes considerable satisfaction in the publication in its monograph series of this study of the work and influence of the Martiniquean poet and political leader, Aimé Césaire.

The author, Susan Frutkin, was among the first group of enrollees in the graduate program of studies established by the Center in 1964. Mrs. Frutkin embarked on her investigations of Césaire's career in preparation of her Master's thesis, carried out under the supervision of Professor Ernst Halperin, then a member of the Center faculty and now with Boston University. Subsequently, Mrs. Frutkin independently continued and expanded her research on Césaire, including periods of study in France and in Martinique.

Secondly, although the Center, like other elements of the University of Miami, has always placed high priority on study programs and research activities relating to the Caribbean, we have tended to concentrate on Spanish-speaking and, more recently, English-speaking areas. Mrs. Frutkin's work on Césaire marks the beginning of what we hope to be increasing emphasis on the other lands and peoples with differing heritages and associations in the region. Beyond all else, however, is the fact that this book focuses on the situation and outlook of Blacks in the Caribbean and constitutes, in our view, a significant contribution to the field of Black Studies.

Perhaps nowhere in the world, other than Africa itself, have Blacks played as great a role in shaping the culture and mode of life of an area as in the islands of the Caribbean. Now Blacks are increasingly emerging as a principal, and in some cases dominant, political force, and any understanding of present and future trends for the region requires close attention to their aspirations and activities. Moreover, and this is particularly important for this country, Blacks of the Caribbean are exerting mounting influence on Black movements in other parts of the world.

Aimé Césaire is perhaps the outstanding example of this last phenomenon, and it is on this aspect of his career that Mrs. Frutkin centers main attention. She has not attempted a biography of Césaire in the usual sense, but has sought to highlight and analyze his influence, beginning many years back, in generating a sense of Black identity and Black pride in a world dominated by non-Blacks. "Black is beautiful," and the many ramifications that have emerged from this concept, had their origins in the writings and thinking of Césaire. For a period, this extraordinarily sensitive and highly literate leader looked to communism as the means to attain a new lot for his people, both in his homeland and in the world at large. But he came to be repelled by what he felt to be the neo-imperialism inherent in the organized communist movement, and by the vision of a faceless role for Blacks within a proletarian order on the Soviet model. He has since shifted his dedication and the power of his intellect and literary talents to an equal place for Blacks as Blacks among the world's peoples and societies.

Mose L. Harvey
Director
Center for Advanced International Studies
University of Miami

PREFACE

This small book is the outgrowth of a Master's thesis I wrote at the University of Miami in 1968. I had been looking for a subject which would combine three disparate research interests of mine: international communism, Latin America, and the problem of Blacks in our contemporary society. I was despairing of success when I was reminded of a Caribbean Communist leader who had resigned during the reaction to Hungary in 1956 — and was the only Party chief to do so. It seemed worth pursuing.

It was indeed! The trail led to Aimé Césaire, whose unique character and career not only fulfilled my three requirements but exceeded my expectations in sheer interest and special relevance to today's world.

Césaire's story carries implications far beyond the Caribbean, to Europe, Africa, and back to America. His contribution straddles two cultures, two eras, two careers. His life and work illuminate colonial history, Pan-Africanism, the black power movement, third world diplomacy and modern literature — a few of the unexpected and pleasant surprises which my research held in store for me.

The work on my thesis, "Aimé Césaire: Negro Poet and Martiniquais Political Leader" was difficult. Limited to materials on hand in this country or available through correspondence, I was unable to obtain up-to-date statistics from Martinique, information pertaining to Césaire's political activities on the island or, indeed, any first-hand account of his views on certain vital questions. Government documents and party information located in Martinique and France were unavailable; my first letters to Césaire went unanswered. I therefore confined the original draft of my thesis mainly to Césaire's philosophical and political ideas, extracted in part from his literary works, which I obtained from libraries and bookstores throughout the United States and France.

In January 1969, I was surprised and honored when "Aimé Césaire" was awarded the annual John Barrett Prize for the best thesis in Inter-American studies at the University of Miami. The award, plus the interest shown by many people in this unusual man, inspired me to continue my research. My new objective was to write a book which would contribute to the expanding field of black studies and shed light on the relatively unexplored question of the relationship between communism and "black power."

In the summer of 1971, renewed efforts to interview Césaire bore fruit. He agreed to see me if I was prepared to brave a visit to Martinique in the heat of August, a month which he, as mayor of Fort-de-France, planned to devote to his local constituents.

Expecting the worst from a radical French intellectual, who referred to the United States as the "white dog of the North," I approached my first meeting with Césaire with some trepidation and a tape recorder. It was an oppressively hot, humid day. I made my way on foot through narrow city streets choked with cars, boutiques and people.

The mayoralty was all that I had imagined: a colonial edifice, white stuccoed and heavy; the interior, unpretentious, save for the long staircase leading upstairs. It was not difficult to find the mayor's office: a noisy crowd on a landing outside was an unmistakable guide. An iron grate separated the constituents from a large anteroom, where a conference table, a score of chairs and several young men in khaki stood in disarray.

In spite of my appointment, I was fully prepared to be preempted by the waiting crowd. I was wrong. Within minutes, one of his entourage ushered me in to see Monsieur Le Maire.

If I had any fears of hostility on Césaire's part, he put them immediately to rest. As he rose to greet me, a broad grin broke across his face.

"Well, what does the American lady want to see me about?" he said, slightly bemused and condescending, but far from hostile.

That first interview lasted about an hour and a half. Since Césaire's manner betrayed a tolerance mixed with impatience, I got right down to business. He responded to my most searching questions matter-of-factly, as though taking stock. I jotted down notes; the tape recorder lay passively on the desk, otherwise cluttered with hand-carved Martiniquais artifacts.

Césaire was, himself, a bit of a surprise. He is short and round, but gives the impression of being large, with well-defined features. His eyes are intelligent, alert, penetrating. His voice is rich, cultured, soft-spoken. He is very black.

I returned the next day to discuss, in depth, various questions I had laid out the day before, but which we had only been able to touch upon. Again, there was the crowd outside his door, his faithful entourage, and street sounds from the city pouring through the open windows. Again, he wore his dark, overlarge, incongruous business suit. But he was at home in his small, stark room and definitely more relaxed.

After granting permission to turn on my tape recorder, Césaire addressed my questions. I was relieved that he was so responsive — it is the ever-present teacher in him. Poetic in speech and practiced in the art of diplomacy, Césaire is a master at the French language.

While his manner is generally gentle and cordial, he is very proud, indignant at injustice and defensive about his people's plight. He holds his views strongly. In spite of his pride and intellectual power, however, Césaire was human enough to appear flattered by the interest in him which my visit represented. His warmth and wit were evident in his inscription scrawled in my copy of his "Cahier d'un Retour Au Pays Natal:"

> Pour Mme. Suzanne . . . qui m'a posé tant de questions aimablement perfides . . . avec toute ma sympathie . . . Aimé Césaire

He is a human being first. He is a poet, too. And then only, perhaps, is he a politician.

I rounded out my several days in Martinique gathering statistical data, hearing others' impressions of Césaire and understanding why people return day after day to wait outside his door, like so many moths around a light.

*   *   *   *   *   *

For his wisdom and patience in directing my original Master's thesis on Aimé Césaire, I owe a debt of gratitude to Dr. Ernst Halperin. And for encouraging me to develop and publish this book, I owe another great debt to Dr. Mose Harvey.

I
THE MAN — Soft Voice, Loud Echo

This is a study of the Martiniquais, Aimé Césaire, black poet and political leader. He is an exceptional product of the colonial experience and a prophet of his race in the modern world. His influence transcends the narrow limits of his island home and reaches beyond his even wider reading public.

Father of "négritude," Césaire has given the black power and black nationalist movements the world over a point of departure, a common language, a feeling of solidarity. His basic philosophical concepts are present in the rhetoric of the current racial upheavals in the United States and they feed the revolutionary changes taking place throughout the black world of Africa and the Caribbean.

"Négritude," says Césaire, "is the affirmation that one is black and proud of it."[1] When he first gave expression to this idea in the thirties, it was no less than revolutionary. Today, it is widely accepted as a natural and integral part of the black ethos.

Though not well-travelled, Césaire is well-known and admired by blacks of the Western Hemisphere. Eldridge Cleaver has called him "one of the greatest black writers of the Twentieth Century."[2] Césaire has also been a moving force in the Pan African movement and is a consistently compelling figure at international gatherings of black personalities. At one such conference of black writers and artists, James Baldwin described a speech of Césaire as the day's "great event . . . very brilliantly delivered."[3]

As an intellectual and as a Negro, Césaire has always assumed he has a responsibility of leadership in the black world. He considers himself a poet first, but he has been a teacher, a politician, an historian and a playwright.

At times, Césaire has been inspired. He has also been conspiciously inconsistent. Essentially a non-political person, Césaire nevertheless ventured into politics right after the war as leader of the Communist Party of Martinique, from which he resigned a decade later to form his own independent political party. He has firmly denounced the imposition of European solutions on the underdeveloped countries, but he is a long-standing fixture of the French parliamentary system and has often voted for the extension of French economic and social laws to the island. He believes in the validity of even the smallest national entity, but he does not advocate independence for his own beloved Martinique. He has both staunchly supported and actively rejected French departmental status for the island. At home, he is considered too radical by

[1]From my interview with Aimé Césaire in his office in the Mairie, Fort-de-France, Martinique, August, 1971. Subsequently cited as "My interview."
[2]Eldridge Cleaver, *Soul on Ice*, (New York: Dell Publishing Co. Inc., 1968), p. 102.
[3]James Baldwin, *Nobody Knows My Name*, (New York: Dell, 1961), pp. 38-41.

some and not radical enough by others, but his personal prestige among both groups is legendary. He vehemently denounces the French policy of assimilation and at the same time is himself the most eloquent testimony to whatever success that policy might have had.

Aimé Césaire is relevant today on many levels. His paradoxical career illuminates the desperate and complicated struggle by colored peoples everywhere to establish an identity, to assert themselves and to achieve a new dignity. In particular, Césaire's unique experience with communism affords us an opportunity to scrutinize the relationship between "négritude" and communism.

Moreover, Césaire is the most influential, if not the only popular political leader in the French Antilles, part of the chain of islands strung out in the Caribbean sea between the United States mainland and South America. Martinique is, itself, of interest. Today, more than ever, she is an island of historical paradox and modern problems. Politically, economically and institutionally, she is part of France; geographically and psychologically, she is Caribbean. As a full-fledged department of France, her people are citizens of the Republic, she has a berth in the Common Market, her cultural heritage includes the French Revolution and General de Gaulle and she has a standard of welfare living well beyond her means. But she also belongs inescapably to the so-called "third world:" ex-colonial, undeveloped, of predominantly African and ex-slave heritage, in the midst of an agonizing national reappraisal.

It is the Martiniquais' resulting identity crisis for which Aimé Césaire speaks. And while Martinique's historical relationship with France lends that crisis special character, the struggle for national identity is a universal cause in the ex-colonial world today.

This study, therefore, examines both Aimé Césaire and Martinique. It considers 1) "négritude" and its natural corollary, "black nationalism," 2) their incompatibility with communism, 3) the anti-French and anti-European posture of a black intellectual heir to the French revolutionary tradition which established "liberté, égalité, fraternité" as national values, 4) Césaire's position as a black leader, and 5) Martinique itself and, within the broader frame of reference of the Caribbean, the "third world."

II
MARTINIQUE — The Context

Martinique is a volcanic, tropical island of 660 square miles. She basks in the Caribbean sea, where quiet beauty belies a tumultuous past and small islands have been battered by the vicissitudes of history.

As with many of the Caribbean islands, Martinique was shuttled back and forth for two centuries between the great colonial powers, England and France, a pawn in their numerous wars. In 1814, she was returned to France definitively.

For more than three hundred years, however, the development of Martinique was largely a function of French colonial rule, which tended toward centralization and assimilation.[1] This double-pronged approach served both to extend French influence and to reinforce French power well beyond her own borders.

Centralization was rigidly institutionalized in France: all power emanated from Paris; all focus of public life in the colonies was directed toward the capital. At the same time, assimilation implied integration in a broad sense, well beyond the political and economic context. The French characteristically attempted to assimilate every inhabitant of their colonies, and, to this end, they consciously superimposed French culture, traditions and social values on the native societies, no matter how diverse or far-flung. The presumption was that the colonies would eventually be fully incorporated in the body politic.

As a result, France evolved a unique relationship with her colonies based on classical colonial exploitation mixed with self-serving liberalism. Most of the laws of the land, the rights of citizens and certainly all major changes in France were either immediately reflected in or directly applied to the territories. But at best, the colonies were merely the creature of French national policies as conceived in Paris; their economies were geared deliberately to serve metropolitan needs, and their only significant distinction lay in the degree to which they bore evidence of French influence.

Soon after they first came to Martinique in 1635, the French rapidly exterminated the indigenous Indians, introduced the African slave trade, and renounced subsistence farming in favor of a monoculture plantation system based on sugar cane. From then on, Martinique functioned economically as a typical "colonial pacte" trading partner: she supplied sugar to France; France supplied all else to Martinique.

---

[1] In contrast to the British colonial policy which encourages decentralization and internal autonomy. Daniel Guérin, *The West Indies and Their Future*, trans. by Austryn Wainhouse (London: Dobson Books, Ltd., 1961), p. 144.

On the other side of the coin, slavery was abolished in Martinique, in spite of strenuous planter objections, in 1848, the year of its abolition in metropolitan France. While the island was under the powerful jurisdiction of a metropolitan governor, a decree of 1848 assured Martinique a representation of two deputies and one senator in the French Parlement. In 1870 universal suffrage was granted.

Carrying the assimilation process still further, the French introduced compulsory education in their colonies. As a result, Martinique has always enjoyed a high literacy rate; it has also always had a thoroughly French educational system. To this day, French is taught as the "first" language, while the local Creole is suppressed and even denigrated; French history and literature take precedence over those of the island; even French geography is emphasized.[2]

The degree to which assimilation has been effected is evident today in the fact that the daily newspapers, movies and television arrive in Martinique from Paris along with the meat, wine (the island is rum-producing) and fashions. The streets of Fort-de-France (Martinique's capital) are as jammed with French automobiles, bought on credit, as the streets of Paris. Vacationing in "the South" means going to the Riviera; discussions of theater revolve around the Paris stage; team scores from France are as avidly followed as the local cock-fight results. Clearly, French culture and civilization, habits, dress and social values have characterized and shaped the life of the island.

Significantly, after a century of citizenship and intense assimilation, the vast majority of Martinique's population is demonstrably proud of and loyal to the French association. The Martiniquais has enjoyed thinking of himself as French first — not black, African, Caribbean or even Martiniquais. When the Fourth French Republic submitted the question of the territories' future status to a plebescite in 1946, the Martiniquais overwhelmingly voted to become a department of France. When de Gaulle visited the island in 1964 and told the throngs that came to greet him "You are so French!" the cheering was uncontrollable.

But the unique relationship with France has been a mixed blessing and accounts to a large degree for many of Martinique's current ills. Most of the islanders appreciate the benefits, the security and the prestige which the relationship with France affords, but the classical inequities of the colonial exploitation have not been erased and the self-evident, non-European ancestry

---

[2] Martinique's educational system has compulsory primary schooling; separate (boys and girls) lycées are available. There are two technical colleges and the Institut Henri Vizioz offers law, politics and economics. Seventy-five percent of adults and ninety-five percent of school children are literate. The discrepancy is due to the fact that while education is compulsory from ages 6-14, up to 8,000 students drop out each year in Fort-de-France alone. Many adults have simply forgotten how to read. Ambassade de France, *Martinique: Pearl of the Antilles* (New York: Service de Presse et d'Information, October, 1961), p. 10. Interview with Renaud de Grandmaison, Executive Secretary to Césaire.

4

of the vast majority of Martiniquais is everywhere apparent to the naked eye. There are also obvious practical problems inherent in the situation, since a tropical island, by definition, faces problems different in the extreme from those of metropolitan France.

The application of metropolitan laws, the assertion of power and the disinterest required in solving the huge problems of such a small outpost have produced some predictable anomalies.

Since the 1946 plebesçite, Martinique has been an "overseas department" of France. As such, she has the same status as Seine, Savoie or any of the other provinces of European France. Correspondingly, the seat of her national government is in Paris, 5,000 miles away.

The island is divided into two arrondissements, with eight cantons, thirty-two communes; she sends three deputies to the Chambre des Députés in France, two to the Sénat, and one to the Conseil Economique. In general, community affairs are run by locally-elected officials. However, because of France's high degree of centralization, all effective legislative, administrative and judicial authority for the island ultimately reside in Paris. All French laws passed in the National Assembly are automatically applicable to the island, unless a specific exception is inserted into the law. Most of France's extensive social and labor legislation has, therefore, been applied to Martinique to some degree; wages have been boosted to comply with French laws; the island's budget has become integrated into the central government's; taxes, at the same rate as in the metropole, are levied by and paid to central revenue; the Antillean franc has been aligned with the French franc.

The French government is represented in Martinique by a prefect, who has the power to declare an emergency and the responsibility for the defense and security of the island. For the most part, however, he simply administers decisions made in Paris.

Three far-reaching political difficulties have arisen as a result of departmentalization. First, the island's representatives, who once exerted some influence through their own Minister, now each exercise only 1/600th of the power and authority of the National Assembly. Since the central government has jurisdiction over most matters, the influence of a local majority, which might be easy to obtain, is often negated through lack of a majority in the National Assembly. The consequence is often a conflict between the representatives of Martinique and the metropolitan ministers who have no familiarity with the island's diverse problems.[3]

---

[3]See Georges Spitz, *"La Martinique et Ses Institutions Depuis 1948,"* *Developments Towards Self-Government in the Caribbean,* (The Hague: W. Van Hoeve, Ltd., 1955) p. 114, and Guérin, *The West Indies and Their Future, p. 152.*

Secondly, the authority of the prefects, their relationship with the local officials and the exercise of their police powers has been a consistent source of discontent. True, the prefect of Martinique, in theory, has no more power than the prefect of any other department of France, but in fact, the conversion of the representative of metropolitan France on the island from colonial governor to prefect seems to be in name only. The prefect usually remains aloof from the population and at odds with the local government officials. His power, in good part due to his control over the civilian security forces, is resented for its use in putting down any demonstration against the central government's policies; his control over the press and television rankles the intellectuals; his office is more feared than revered by the native population.

Finally, departmentalization has opened the floodgates of the pervasive French bureaucracy, creating a problem that imposes itself on many aspects of Martiniquais life. Not only does it contribute to racial friction, in general, but it also creates dissatisfaction among the local colored bourgeoisie, which had traditionally occupied the middle and lower ranks of the island's administration. In addition, the bureaucracy's inflated salaries and demands for foreign products have been some of the major contributing factors to the serious dislocations in Martinique's economy.

While many who voted for departmentalization in 1946 did so out of patriotism or the urge to have concrete recognition of their status as French citizens, many also did so in the hope of improving the island's economic outlook. Unfortunately, departmentalization has done very little, if anything, to improve Martinique's economic situation; it may even have exacerbated the problems.

Martinique's economy is, in fact, characterized by gross disequilibrium. The historical bases of the problem can be traced to the old system of "pacte colonial," by which the colony was established as a monoculture economy. Characteristically, Martinique's function was to provide sugarcane and its by-products to France, while acting at the same time as an exclusive market for French products, carried in French ships. Martinique often paid a premium for products which might have been purchased cheaper elsewhere. As a corollary, the island was prevented from producing anything for herself.

Inevitably, Martinique's economy developed with absolute primacy of the agricultural sector, and more specifically, of one or two agricultural products. As late as 1960, with the small addition of bananas and pineapples, sugarcane and its products still accounted for 97% of Martinique's exports.[4]

---

[4]*Martinique: Pearl of the Antilles*, p. 6. Mr. Murch in his dissertation quotes this figure as 98% in 1965. *Political Integration As An Alternative to Independence in the French Antilles* (Ann Arbor: University Microfilms, Inc., 1968), p. 27.

The picture is only slightly different today; the value of bananas exported is now almost double that of sugar and rum.[5] Unfortunately, however, more than reflecting any great success in diversifying agricultural production, these figures reflect a deterioration of the sugar sector in Martinique which has reached crisis proportions.

The crisis is illustrated by the fact that between 1965 and 1970, sugarcane production dropped from 70,000 tons to 27,000 tons. (The capacity is 110,000 tons; the quota for exportation to France is 70,000.) Only six of the former 15 refineries remain in operation.[6]

Wage levels have played a role here as well as in other sectors of the economy. The farm hand, for example, gets a legal minimum of 2.79 FF per hour (compared to 3.27 FF per hour in France). This represents more than three times what the same worker would get in the Ivory Coast and other countries with competitive products.[7]

Yet, in spite of the increased wages, or maybe because of them, sugar cane workers work more and more sporadically and many are leaving the fields for easier, less stigmatized work, less seasonal work, or just for the big cities.

These labor problems discourage the Martiniquais sugar planter from replanting. Moreover, France's sugar subsidy system permits the sugar cane planter to sell the part of his quota which he has not produced to metropolitan sugar beet producers, who may then sell an equal part of their production at sugar cane prices.[8]

The upshot is that Martinique, although by definition an agricultural economy, is nevertheless a long way from providing for her own subsistence. Besides sugar cane and bananas, Martinique grows and exports pineapples and a small amount of flowers and fresh vegetables. But efforts to introduce other subsistence food crops, as well as cattle raising and fishing, have been essentially unsuccessful. The extensive list of Martinique's imports includes such items as meat, fish, butter, fresh vegetables, fruit juice, tobacco, flour, coffee, as well as all canned goods, chemical products, manufactures, etc. In 1969, Martinique imported 128 million FF worth of foodstuffs, over 1/3 of her total of consumer goods imports, which amounted to 347 million FF.[9]

[5] M. Ernoult, Chief of the Départment D'Agriculture, Martinique, in an interview, August, 1971, gave figures for 1969 as 100 million FF (bananas) vs. 46 million FF (sugar). The Direction Générale des Douanes put the figures at 83 million FF vs. 41 million FF in 1970.
[6] *Institut D'Emission Des Départements D'Outre-Mer: rapport d'activité*, Exercice 1969 (Paris: Siége Social, 19), pp. 18-19 also p. 3b from statistical reports.
[7] This January 1, 1970 figure on wages represents an increase of 13.30% since January 1, 1969, *Institut D'Emission*, p. 49.
[8] *Le Monde Diplomatique*, October 1971, p. 17.
[9] *Institut D'Emission, op. cit.* p. 44.

Although in theory it has been abandoned, other vestiges of the "pacte coloniale" clearly remain in the department's economic relationship with France. Their continued existence is effected through tariffs and customs charges and to no less a degree by huge sugar subsidies, which France underwrites at almost three times world market prices. Evidence of the continuing policy can readily be seen in Martinique's excessive unfavorable trade balance.

In 1970, for example, Martinique's total imports rose to 810,608,000 FF, of which 600,301,000 FF were from France or other franc countries. In the same year, the island's exports dropped to a total of 166,827,000 FF of which 159,677,000 FF worth were sent to France and other franc countries.[10]

For a few years just before World War II, liberalized trade laws were in operation and Martinique's economy was relatively stable and prosperous; the sugar planters were assured of a ready market in metropolitan France, while they were able to import at considerably lower prices from the United States. In fact, Martinique's balance of payments at that time showed a steady increase on the plus side.[11] But the effects of the war and France's subsequent return to protectionist policies reversed the trend.

The excessive concentration of landed property in the hands of the white élite on the island is another significant by-product of the plantation economy. As late as 1935, 3% of the land-owning population (or 208 proprietors) owned 61% of the cultivable soil; 5% (or 365 proprietors) owned 75%; while 72% of the landowners (or 4,696) owned 7% of the cultivable land (under 3 hectares each). During the sixties, some 3,200-3,500 hectares (out of a total of 46,000 cultivable hectares) were redistributed under what passed for land reform.[12] In the previous 25 years, a total of 2,000-3,000 hectares had been redistributed. The central government's attempts at land reform had been hampered not only by the size of the task, but also by its inherent sensitivity and the fear that agriculture would come to a complete standstill were it not for the large proprietors.[13]

The most conspicuous fact of Martiniquais economic life today is the influx of funds from the central budget. "The primary resource of the island,"

[10] 1970 Statistical reports of the office of Départements D'Outre-Mer, "Martinique." p. 6b and 8b.

[11] *Le Monde,* January 19, 1954, p. 4.

[12] Guérin, *The West Indies and Their Future,* pp. 37-38. *Le Monde* article of September 11, 1962, p. 8, column 3, indicates similar figures: 3% of landowners owning 74%, while 90% own under 5 hectares each—the date of these figures is not given. M. Ernoult of the agriculture department estimated the figures given for land reform.

[13] Murch claims that between 1962-1965, some 4,000 hectares of land were purchased by the state and distributed to 1,282 families. (*op.cit.*, p. 44). Césaire, in November 1963, accused the government of having allotted only 200 million francs for land reform when 6 billion would be necessary, in addition to which, not one large estate had been dismantled up to that time. *Le Monde,* October 30, 1963. M. Ernoult pointed out that 65% of the sugar cane is still produced by large property holders, 10% by medium size property holders (5-30 hectares) and 25% by small land holders. Sugar cane is grown most economically on large estates.

8

quipped the well-known French magazine, *L'Express,* "is the Budget of France. It accounts for more than half of Martinique's revenue."[14]

In concrete terms, the 1970 figures show that public financing in Martinique rose to 864 million FF of which 527 million FF were contributed directly by metropolitan funds. (The rest were raised through taxes and assessments on the island.) In addition, some 644,500,000 FF in credits were extended to the private sector and 300,100,000 FF to the public sector in metropolitan funds.[15]

The three main channels of distribution of these funds are through bureaucratic salaries, credits to carry out various ministerial projects or special overseas department's investment funds (FIDOM) and aid in the form of subsidies and grants.

While the infusion of metropolitan funds into the Martiniquais economy has raised the standard of living, improved the island's infrastructure (roads, utilities, etc.) and provided badly needed social services, the overall economy, by standard measures of growth and strength, may actually have deteriorated in the process. As a consequence, Césaire and others have characterized Martinique as becoming progressively more underdeveloped.

The root problem is that French assistance has been along social rather than developmental lines, and, while a higher standard of living has accompanied the infusion of public funds, in reality it reflects an inflated state of welfare living rather than any improvement in the island's productive capabilities.

Welfare, of course, has done nothing to discourage the population's historic indolence. Nor has it checked the movement from farm to city, where the government provides an easy way out with family allocations which go a long way to providing basic needs in Martinique's subtropical climate. In addition, a policy of family allowances in a country of severe over-population and high birth rate has been less than practical.

Unfortunately, a large part of the public funds sent to Martinique are spent on the bureaucracy, which itself administers the funds and which receives 50% of the salaries paid, while making up only 10% of the working population. In addition, the bureaucracy earns 40% more than it would in metropolitan France. This fact alone helps to keep the cost of living on the island at 40-50% above that in France. This, in turn, introduces disequilibrium into the salary structures of private enterprise and creates jealousies among the non-bureaucrats.[16]

---

[14]*L'Express,* August 3-9, 1970, p. 55.

[15]*Institut D'Emission, op.cit.,* pp. 69-75.

[16]*Le Monde Diplomatique,* October 1971, p. 17. Also my interview with Louis Lepouliquen, Editor in Chief of *France-Antilles,* August 1971.

Finally, the anomalous economic relationship between France and Martinique entails the return of a large proportion of the government's funds in the form of payments for imports — necessarily from metropolitan France. According to one statistic, for each 1000 FF of public expenditure, 500 francs are spent for imports.[17]

Industry, which was effectively prohibited on the island in colonial days, is badly needed to counterbalance the overdependence on agriculture and France and make Martinique more economically viable. Unfortunately, it has been discouraged rather than attracted investment on the island. In spite of some tax incentives, production costs are very high due to the lack of resources and energy as well as relatively high salary levels. In addition, there is the impossibility of competing with French — now Common Market — products. Investors, therefore, either go elsewhere or enter commerce or tourism.[18]

If some local authorities are proud of the new oil refinery built in Martinique (as well as a future cement plant), more realistic observers find it an object of derision. Not only does it make no contribution toward the island's self-sufficiency (it has virtually no market on the island), but it employs a maximum of 100 persons, while tens of thousands of jobs are needed.[19]

The gloomy outlook for industrialization is matched only by the discouraging trends in agriculture illustrated by the decline in sugar cane production, described above.

The overall economic picture, therefore, is one of an overdependence on France for trade, funds, and social benefits, in conjunction with an inordinately high cost of living, a debilitating lack of initiative and dynamism on the local level, a disrupting imbalance in the various sectors of the economy, and a French policy which covers up rather than builds up.

Intensifying this seeming economic impasse are the endemic population problems. Over 340,000 people now live on the 660 square miles of the island, and the population increases at a rate of 3½% per year. There is also extreme density of population — both on the cultivable soil and in the capital of Fort-de-France, where nearly one-third of the island's population lives.[20]

These factors plus the general state of the economy result in extensive unemployment. Some estimates range from one-third to 70% of the working population (100,000-120,000 people) either totally or partially out of work or not even actively looking for employment.[21] Of those that work, only a very

---

[17]Ibid., and Institut D'Emission, op. cit., p. 11.

[18]See Le Monde, August 27, 1970. p. 6.

[19]In my interview with Lepouliquen, he said the refinery is "ridiculous" and tourism is "nonsense" . . . what the island needs is artisanal work. Also, L'Express, op. cit., p. 55.

[20]Between 1901 and 1946, the population of Fort-de-France tripled. Actual density figures for the whole island given by Guérin, op. cit. are 696 per square mile (270 per km²) compared to 192 per square mile (74 per km²) in metropolitan France. Also my interview with M. Ernoult.

[21]Le Monde, August 27, 1970, p. 6.

small percentage do so steadily, while the vast majority work sporadically or at seasonal jobs. Fortunately, many in this latter group own a small plot of land from which their subsistence is assured.

Economic development and, specifically, industrialization would alleviate the severe scarcity of jobs, but as seen above, there has been virtually no progress along these lines.

High French officials admit that the demographic-unemployment problem is the number one plague in the overseas department of Martinique. Attempts at family planning have been made, but while the 1969 increase in the population was down to 2.3%, it represents only a slight decline over previous years. The problem remains urgent.[22]

It is of particular significance for Martinique's political complexion that over half of the population is under twenty years old.[23] The lack of economic opportunities on the island for Martinique's relatively well-educated youth has led to a restless, disgruntled and potentially explosive generation.

Emigration to France has been the traditional outlet for the island's frustrated young. Unfortunately, it has produced some undesirable side effects. Not only does it have a tendency to drain off the most dynamic elements, many of whom are those who simply never return after completing their studies in metropolitan France, but it leaves a still rather large, unfulfilled group on the island to vent its feelings in sporadic incidents against the government.

In 1963, in an effort "to contribute toward limiting the expansion of the population,"[24] and thus create a controlled safety valve for the increasing numbers of unemployed and dissatisfied citizens in the overseas departments, the central government established a Bureau for the Development of Migrations from the Overseas Departments (BUMIDOM).

Since its inception, BUMIDOM has brought about 2400 Martiniquais to the metropolitan area every year. There, some attempt is made to get them established within the work force, but the character of those migrating through the Bureau is radically different from those who go on their own. Many end up as third-class citizens, often more aware of their blackness, more confused as to their identity and susceptible to radicalization.

At the same time, in Martinique, this French policy of planned migration is coming under more and more frequent attack. Some flatly call it a "policy of deportation."[25] Many see it as an undisguised attempt to palliate the politi-

---

[22] In my interview with Jean Terrade, Prefect for Martinique, he claimed, "The Martiniquais woman is awakening" to the efforts of family planning. Figures don't show much progress, however. He said a stabilized population of 400,000 would be "ideal."

[23] *Le Monde,* January 19, 1954, p. 2 and Guérin, *The West Indies and Their Future,* pp. 27-28. Compare to 43.9% under 19 in 1946; 40% under 15 in most of the Antilles in 1950, and 27% under 20 in the U.S. The figures are about the same or worse today.

[24] *Institut D'Emission, op. cit.,* p. 49.

[25] Camille Darsiéres, *Rapports De 3ème Congrès,* (Fort-de-France, August 12-13, 1967), pp. 4-6.

11

cal and economic problems of the department. It is obvious, in any case, that emigration has done nothing to improve conditions on the island itself.

The most central and disturbing feature of the demographic problem is the social structuring of the population. Martinique has not been exempt from "the most obvious fact of Caribbean life, that there is a basic causal connection between color, class and ownership and that the three things form a single social pattern."[26] The peculiar Martiniquais expression of this pattern was forged by the dual heritage of French colonial rule and African slave trade:

> If the French have exported their civilization to Martinique they have also exported their social structure. The hard social prejudices of the metropolitan bourgeoisie have coalesced with the racial distinctions derived from slavery to produce the most organized society in the West Indies.[27]

Practically speaking, Martinique's society is made up of three color groups: the whites or Creoles (called békés) with European heritage; the mulattoes or browns, of mixed blood; and the blacks, or nearly pure Negroes of African (and usually slave) descent.

Although there has not been legal segregation or discrimination in Martinique, *de facto* racial prejudice was always a fact of Martiniquais social life. The white Creole society (of 2,000-3,000 people, less than one percent of the population) has been traditionally closed and disdainful of all outsiders. Its claim to preeminence is based on economic control; local political power having been ceded, in the wake of universal suffrage, to the numerically stronger colored elements. Even when relations with mulattoes are established for business reasons, they seldom if ever, extend to the social level. The mulatto group itself represents a kind of bourgeoisie of color; it includes the professional men, politicians, bureaucrats, businessmen and significantly, the intellectual élite.

Since there is a premium placed on lightness of skin, it has also been true that "racial discrimination operates within coloured society itself."[28] At the bottom of the scale, of course, are the blacks who make up the masses, living in hopeless misery and despair.

Two outstanding features, therefore, have characterized Martinique's social-racial situation: (1) In general, the scale of wealth and social position both correspond inversely to the amount of color in the skin; and (2) While the colored people generally have suffered no outward demonstration of racism by the whites, the more subtle manifestations of prejudice have existed at

---

[26] Paul Blanshard, *Democracy and Empire in the Caribbean* (New York: The MacMillan Company, 1947), p. 51.

[27] Naipaul, *The Middle Passage, op. cit.,* p. 197.

[28] Guérin, *The West Indies and Their Future, op. cit.,* p. 72.

all levels. In Martinique, there is a saying, still quoted today: "The Béké hates the Negro; the mulatto dreams of being white, the black of whitening."[29]

World War II and its concomitant upheavals proved, however, to be a turning point on the island. Of its significant and far-reaching effects on Martinique, not the least was a qualitative change in racial attitudes.

Before 1939, the white békés in Martinique were at least integrated into the economic life of the island and were interested in its welfare. With the fall of France, however, a tyrannical Vichyist governor in the person of Admiral Georges Robert was installed to rule the island. The brunt of his repressive disciplinary methods was borne mainly by the colored community; the social conservatives (planters and churchmen) rallied to his support. Aggravating the situation still further was the arrival of two shiploads of sailors, inundating Fort-de-France alone with almost 10,000 Europeans who, according to one observer, were "of an assured, but previously latent racist mentality."[30] In the four years during which they were locked in Martinique by the allied blockade, they shattered the *modus vivendi* by treating the Antillean as a Negro, rather than as the Frenchman he preferred to consider himself, and by introducing overt racist indignities where none had previously existed. Their presence also caused an acute housing problem. Simultaneously, the war itself was reflected in Martinique, the United States' blockade dealing a ruinous blow to the island's economy. Most significant in the long run, perhaps, was the fact that the extension of the war and its effects to Martinique brought the island into the mainstream of world events.

The infusion of these antagonistic elements, says Frantz Fanon, a Martiniquais radical intellectual, had the interesting effect of forcing the colored population to defend itself for the first time. Irritation and fatigue with the wartime situation on the island rallied the colored population in a united effort for the Free French movement. Massive demonstrations took place in July and August, 1943. This show of strength aided in forcing Admiral Robert to resign in favor of Henri-Étienne Hoppenot, appointed by the Free French Committee of National Liberation, and in effect, says Fanon, "systemized for the first time [the Negro's] political consciousness."[31]

As Fanon implies, underlying this new-found political consciousness was the even more powerful motivating force of a growing, specifically "black" consciousness. And to the degree that the racial consciousness developed, there was a tendency on the island for class antagonisms and political attitudes to cut across traditionally rigid color lines at all levels (except within the

---

[29]Quoted in *Le Monde*, January 11, 1962, p. 8, col. 4. (My translation.)
[30]Frantz Fanon, "Antillais et Africains," *Esprit*, February, 1955, p. 265. (My translation.)
[31]*Ibid.*

13

small white minority). Emerging as the dynamic leaders of this changing political and social scene were the mulattoes. In addition, a few of the dark-skinned petty-bourgeoisie who had managed to continue their education and rise out of their wretched surroundings joined the colored, "middleclass" elements. Those who best understood the essence of their subjection in the system, therefore, fused into an aggressive vanguard agitating for an end not only to wartime occupation but also to the indignities of their racial subjugation and ultimately the system underlying it. The inspiration, guiding light, and spokesman for this newly articulate group was Aimé Césaire, father of "négritude."

III
NÉGRITUDE — Black and Proud

Aimé Césaire was born in Basse Pointe, Martinique, on June 25, 1913, the son of a poor black family. Césaire himself has described his early life:

> In the early morning another small malodorous house in a very narrow road a tiny house which shelters in its innards of rotten wood dozens of rats and the turbulence of my six brothers and sisters, a cruel little house whose harshness troubles us each month until payday and my strange father gnawed by one great sorrow, I have never known which, moved by some unpredictable witchcraft to melancholy tenderness or violent rage; and my mother whose legs pedal for our insatiable hunger, pedal day and night, I am even awakened nights by these tireless legs which tread the night and by the noise of a Singer which bites into the soft flesh of the night while my mother pedals, pedals night and day for our hunger.[1]

In contrast to the deprivation of his living conditions, however, Césaire received the best public education made available by the French system. In 1931, at the age of eighteen, after graduating from the Lycée Schoelcher, where he was imbued with the whole gamut of French cultural values, he went to Paris on a scholarship to continue his studies at the Ecole Normale Supérieure. The prestige of this institute of higher learning among French intellectuals stems not only from the keen competition for admittance, but also from the fact that it is the font of the most sophisticated French ideas, geared to the training of professors of sciences and letters and known for its celebrated graduates. To be a "normalien" in France is automatically to belong to a recognized intellectual élite founded in France's prestigious cultural heritage. After receiving his diploma, Césaire became a teacher of literature.

By his own account, the most significant and far-reaching event of Césaire's eight years in Paris was his friendship with co-student Léopold Sédar Senghor, a poet, now president of Senegal. It was Senghor who opened up to him the world of Africa. Its discovery and the close association with Senghor crystallized Césaire's as yet unformulated reasons for hatred of and alienation from Martiniquais society. The relationship led to their collaboration on *L'Etudiant Noir.*

Published in 1935-1936, *L'Etudiant Noir* was a review dedicated to instituting interaction between the Antillean colored and the Black African, based on the common denominator of "négritude."

"Négritude is a point of departure," Césaire explained in a recent interview with the author. "It is the affirmation that one is black and proud of it . . .

---

[1] Aimé Césaire, *Cahier D'Un Retour Au Pays Natal,* (Paris: Présence Africaine, 1956), p. 37. All quotations from this poem are my own translation from the original.

that there is a solidarity between all blacks . . . that we are suspended together in space.''[2]

Proffering a new feeling of self-respect and communal strength, Césaire and Senghor labored to arouse blacks eveywhere to an awareness of their African ancestry and the conviction that their common civilization was inherently worthwhile. The black man, proclaimed Césaire, has a peculiar emotional outlook on life and a share in a culture that is different from, but not inferior to, that of the white world. Through the centuries, the black man was the victim of slavery which dispersed him, colonization which alienated him and assimilation which depersonalized him. In this appalling process, the roots of the black man's civilization were ripped from him and superficially replaced by other alien cultures. The result has been cultural anarchy. The essential thing now was for the black man to rediscover the truth of his being and reestablish his own dignity. Négritude, therefore, did not call for a return to the past, but rather respect for the past and a new dynamic, specifically black, attitude toward the future.

Inspired by the need to speak out against political and cultural assimilation, négritude began as a literary movement. Today, as will be seen below, it goes far beyond that challenge: it lends character, indeed shapes, the extensive black revolt against all forms of subordination. In extreme form, it is the justification for the black cause taking precedence over all others, and even to their exclusion.

His collaboration with Senghor on *L'Etudiant Noir* gave Césaire his first insights into his African heritage and established links between him and other blacks of the literary world. It was in a sense a prelude to his first important work, *Notebook on Returning Home.*

Notebook on Returning Home was written in 1936-1937 when Césaire, a young man of twenty-three, was on vacation at the Dalmatian coast home of his fellow-student Petar Guberina.[3] It is a long, rambling, highly emotional poem of sixty-six pages, replete with extravagant imagery and symbolism. Written in free, unrhymed and irregular verse, with an almost ostentatious display of French vocabulary, it is above all a powerful revolutionary appeal to the black man to assert himself. It is the supreme and original statement of négritude.

The poem was written for a Parisian review, *Volontés,* and went almost undiscovered until several years later when André Breton, ''the high priest

---

[2]Césaire, my interview.

[3]Many sources cite this as having been written in 1939. Only Daniel Guérin in his notes to *Les Antilles Décolonisées* (Paris: Présence Africaine, 1956) claims that it was written in 1936-7 and published only in 1939 (p. 182). Considered one of the authorities on Césaire's works and Negro poetry in general, Guberina is now a professor at the University of Zagreb.

of Surrealism'' published a new edition of it.[4] As a result, many critics characterize *Notebook on Returning Home* and the négritude movement which grew up around it as Surrealist. However, in spite of superficial resemblances, it seems clear that Césaire and negritude were different from and independent of the Surrealist movement.[5] Césaire himself has said that he scarcely knew much about surrealism when he wrote it, but that his own development was going in a similar direction. Surrealism was for Césaire more of a justification and a support than an inspiration. It preached total liberation of the spirit which coincided with and provided a vehicle for Césaire's own call to the black people to reaffirm their true identity. ''I always had the feeling of our [black] particularism, so I wanted to use surrealism as a weapon, while staying faithful to négritude.''[6] It is this loyalty to négritude that transcends all other ingredients of Césaire's poem and dictates their very inclusion in it. For example, the poem extols the values of his African cultural heritage and is at the same time a stirring restatement of African primitivism:

> . . . the rhythm achieves at times the unbelievable power of a tam-tam. This movement is like a call to arms, a signal announcing the rebirth of a cause or of a people, the voice of a sorcerer in incantation . . . of a herald of a new era . . .[7]

In his introduction to *Notebook on Returning Home,* Petar Guberina calls it ''the sublime poetic creation of a black poet who has mastered European philosophy, the French language and the multiple meanings of words as few Europeans have.''[8] And it is hard to overlook the fact that these elements are to be found in the poem, for in spite of himself and his new-found ideology, Césaire is a fine product of the very cultural assimilation process which he deplores.

For Césaire, himself, *Notebook on Returning Home* represented a manifold point of departure. Aside from its obvious declaration of his intention to return home to Martinique, it marked the true inception of his literary career and anticipated certain aspects of his future political career. Further, it represented the first clearcut statement of his decision to disassociate himself from European values.

The three most significant themes in *Notebook on Returning Home* upon which Césaire built his concept of négritude are (1) obsession and identity

---

[4]G. R. Coulthard, *Race and Colour in Caribbean Literature* (London: Oxford University Press, 1962), p. 61.

[5]*Ibid.* See also Janheinz Jahn, ''Aimé Césaire,'' *Black Orpheus* (1958), p. 35. 1969. p. 28.

[6]Aimé Césaire quoted in ''Un Poète Politique: Aimé Césaire,'' *Magazine Littéraire,* No. 36, November 1969. p. 28.

[7]René Piquion, *Négritude* (Port-au-Prince, Haiti: Imprimerie de l'Etat, 1961), p. 236. (My translation.)

[8]Césaire, *Cahier D'Un Retour Au Pays Natal, op. cit.,* pp. 18-19.

with the black man and his heritage of slavery; (2) hatred and rejection of the white world as the perpetrator of slavery, colonialism and racism; (3) confidence in a future of universal fraternity. Alienation and acceptance . . . struggle and reassertion . . . solidarity and hope.

The first of these themes is the cornerstone of négritude: the acceptance of oneself as black and the deep-seated belief in the inherent worth of the black peoples.

> I accept . . . I accept . . . completely, without reservation
> . . . my race that no brew of herbs and flowers could wash away.[9]
>
> . . . .
>
> my négritude is not a stone, its deafness flung against the clamor of day
> my négritude is not a speck of dead water on the dead eye of the earth
> my négritude is neither a tower nor a cathedral
>
> it plunges into the red flesh of the sun
> it plunges into the burning flesh of the sky
> it punctures the oppressive prostration of its rigid patience.[10]

The second theme lays the groundwork for Césaire's revolutionary bent as well as the rationale for rejecting Europe and returning home:

> Listen to the white world
> immensely tired from its enormous effort
> its protesting joints crack under the pitiless stars
> its stiffness of blue steel piercing the mystic flesh
> listen to its victories foretelling its coming defeats
> listen to its grandiloquent excuses for its pitiful stumbling
>
> Have pity for our omniscient and childish conquerors!
>
> Hurray for the bitterness of incarnate tears
> for those who have never discovered anything
> for those who have never conquered anything
>
> Hurray for the joy
> Hurray for the love
> Hurray for the bitterness of incarnate tears.[11]

Césaire is specifically concerned with the enslaved Negro: the sons of Negroes brought from Africa in colonial slave-ships; the subjugated, transplanted, humiliated, alienated black man. It is his identity with this miserable creature of colonialism that is the basis for his particular hatred of the French and American racism, as well as his decision to bypass the newly acclaimed glories of the African past in favor of the undistinguished traditions of Martinique:

> I refuse to accept my posturing as authentic glories.
> And I laugh at my former puerile fantasies.
> No, we have never been amazons of the king of Dahomey, nor princes of Ghana . . . I must confess that we were always rather sorry dishwashers, mediocre bootblacks, at best rather competent

---

[9] *Ibid.*, p. 77.
[10] *Ibid.*, p. 71.
[11] *Ibid.*, pp. 72-73.

witchdoctors and the only indisputable record that we have established is that of endurance under the lash . . .
  And for centuries this land proclaimed that we were brute beasts;
that humanity ends at the doors of the slave pen; . . .[12]

In developing the third theme, Césaire emphasizes universal fraternity and
takes great pains to preclude any accusations that he is advocating an anti-
racist racism:

don't make of me that man of hate for
whom I have only hatred

. . . .
you know that it is not out of hatred for the other races
that I toil for this one race
that what I want is
to liberate it at last
to produce from its consummate intimacy
the succulence of fruits for
the universal hunger
for the universal thirst.[13]

Guberina, for one, accepts Césaire's claim to universalism: "The poet puts
the virtues of his race at the service of the liberation of the whole world."[14]
And Césaire, himself, claims that because his concept of négritude is based
on a common civilization and culture rather than a biological purity of blood,
it is in no way racist.[15] But Césaire's point of departure is clearly based on
his own negative opinion of whites, and for him the world is divided inescapably into white and colored. His angry diatribes against Europe and the entire
white world are vivid testimony to what can only be described as anti-white
racism—tempered and moderated over the years—but in 1937, an aggressive,
violent, angry, if negative, racism.
  Finally a synthesis of these three themes is achieved, and the definitive
statement of the Césaire of 1937 is revealed in a very poetic passage:

And we are on our feet now, my land and I
with windswept hair, my small hand
now in its enormous fist and the power
is not in us, but above us, in
a voice which penetrates the night and the crowd like
the sting of an apocalyptic wasp. And the voice
proclaims that Europe, for centuries
has gorged us with lies and blown us up with pestilence, for it is
not true that man's task is accomplished
that we have nothing to do in the world
that we are parasites in the world
that it is enough for us to catch up with the world
but man's task has only just begun

[12]*Ibid.*, pp. 61-62.

[13]*Ibid.*, p. 75.

[14]*Ibid.*, p. 20.

[15]Aimé Césaire quoted in "Un Poète Politique: Aimé Césaire," *Magazine
Littéraire, op. cit.*, p. 32.

and man still has to conquer every barrier
immobilized in the depths of his fervor
and no race has a monopoly of
beauty, of intelligence and strength
and there is room for all on the field of
victory and we know now that the sun
revolves around our world illuminating only that portion selected by
us and that any star
falls to earth at our command.[16]

Césaire's message is powerful: Europe has lied and spread pestilence, the enslaved peoples are regaining their dignity, their sense of worth and the future will not be monopolized by one predominant race or nation. But just as Césaire's optimism is more of an emotional outcry than a battle plan, *Notebook on Returning Home* cannot be said to reflect any clearcut political ideas, but rather the depths of Césaire's emotions and his fundamental frame of reference.

One historian has characterized *Notebook on Returning Home* as "Marxist verse concerning the warfare between the races and the mistreatment of the Negro for generations."[17] But despite Césaire's impending affiliation with the Communist Party, this is not Marxist verse at all! For Marx, history was defined in terms of class struggles and the antagonisms of society in terms of class antagonisms: "The history of all hitherto existing society is the history of class struggles," said Marx. And modern society was described by Marx as consisting of "two great hostile camps . . . Bourgeoisie and Proletariat."[18] In fact, class struggles were seen as a function of his theory of dialectical materialism and it was almost exclusively the economic relationships between the classes that concerned Marx.

In *Notebook on Returning Home,* however, race is the determining factor, not class: modern history dates not from the division of the world into bourgeoisie and proletariat, but from the inception of colonialism and slavery. In fact, the word "proletarian" is not to be found; "nègre," "négraille," "négritude" abound. Césaire was clearly concerned primarily with the cultural and psychological alienation of his race, hardly touching on the economic implications of colonialism.

Césaire's wholesale rejection of Europe is also inconsistent with Marx. For while Marx exhorted the destruction of the capitalist world, the core of which was Europe, he recognized that the seeds of its own destruction and the rise

---

[16]Césaire, *Cahier D'Un Retour Au Pays Natal. op. cit.,* pp. 82-83.

[17]Shelby T. McCloy, *The Negro in the French West Indies* (Kentucky: University of Kentucky Press, 1966), p. 227.

[18]Karl Marx, *Capital, The Communist Manifesto, and Other Writings* (New York: The Modern Library, 1932), p. 321-322.

of the proletariat existed by virtue of the advanced stage of that society and its industrial development. And the new society which he envisioned was relevant specifically to the European situation.

If *Notebook on Returning Home* cannot adequately be described as Marxist verse, still less does it belong to Communist literature. By its most obvious premise and its very timing it defines a frame of reference and a state of mind which belie any affiliation with the Communist thought of the day. Césaire's declaration of his intention to return home in the year 1937 is significant in itself. In 1937, Europe was on the brink of the holocaust of World War II. Foremost in the minds of almost everyone, and certainly the European intellectuals with whom he associated, were Nazism, Fascism, German racism. European leftist circles were actively seeking alliances against fascism wherever they could. The communists were no less absorbed in the fascist invasion of Abyssinia and the Spanish Civil War. But Césaire, the future Communist Party leader, outspoken Marxist revolutionary, and highly educated Europeanized intellectual, in his first published work, neither mentioned nor even reflected any of these earth-shattering events. Césaire, in effect, turned his back on Europe—both physically and spiritually, to the degree that he chose not only to ignore its vital preoccupations, but to reject completely its cultural heritage, its fundamental value system, and its ideological thought to which Marxism, itself, belongs. (The reasons for this seeming paradox will be discussed in Chapter IV, for they were only made manifest in his writing of 1955.)

The emotional outpouring of *Notebook on Returning Home* demonstrates very clearly that the Césaire of 1937 was in rapport neither with the mainstream of political concern, in general, nor with Communist attitudes, in particular. He was consumed by the issues of colonialism and racism and, what was to him, their logical extension: political and cultural annihilation. *Notebook* is the literary outcry by which he sought to crusade against the travesty.

Viewed from the perspective of the 1970's, when such ideas are readily recognized as fundamental to black thought, it is hard to believe that Césaire was proclaiming the virtually unspeakable in the thirties. Frantz Fanon was not exaggerating when he described the reception of Césaire's revolutionary notions:

> For the first time, a high school professor, apparently a reasonable man, was openly saying to the Antillean society 'it is good and beautiful to be black.' It was absolutely a scandal. Stories were told that he was a little crazy, and his friends tried to make excuses for his supposed illness.
>
> What could be more grotesque, in fact, than an educated man having so misunderstood, among other things, that 'it was most unfortunate to be black,' and claiming that his skin is beautiful and that 'the great black pit' is a source of truth? . . . Two centuries of white

truth proved him wrong. He must be crazy, because there could be no question that he wasn't sane.[19]

Since World War II, a new racial consciousness has swept the black world, manifested in a variety of forms. From Lumumba in the Congo to Angela Davis in California; from the Rastafarians in Jamaica to the now scattered Black Panthers, there is a common sympathy shaped by négritude. In the past ten years, Black Power groups have sprung up in almost every country with a sizable black population. While they differ radically from one locale to another, they are all rooted in the basic tenets of négritude.

Négritude also provided one of the philosophical pillars of the awakening of black nationalism: Pan Africanism owes a debt to négritude as do many of the national independence movements in the Caribbean. Within three decades, the basic concepts of négritude have become so fundamental to the mainstream of black thought that they may well be the only unifying force in the otherwise highly fragmented and diversified movement.

In the United States, for example, all the ingredients of négritude can be found to some degree in the many groups within the black movement. The mystique of a common African heritage pervades the black world. Many blacks sport African-style clothes (such as the colorful 'dashiki'), African jewelry and Afro hairstyles, worn by both men and women. Many others have followed the example of author LeRoi Jones, who has assumed the African name of Imamu Amiri Baraka. American blacks have adopted African art forms, music, dance and literature and transformed them into the unique Afro-American 'soul.'

Also common to today's black power movements is the universal disdain for white racism and oppression and a basic rejection of the white world. One extreme is the street cry of 'kill the white pigs.' More sublime is the statement by the Rev. Jesse Jackson, formerly of the Southern Christian Leadership Conference, now head of PUSH, scornfully denouncing the white man's inherent racism with the observation that 'pinkskin worship is pathological and ought to be dealt with by psychotherapists, not politicians.'[20]

The recent formation of an ambitious, if fragile, new political movement of blacks in the United States indicates that the black community has come a long way in developing a race-based attitude in the face of a white-run society.

"The Democrats can no longer take us for granted, while the Republicans write us off," declared Jackson at the first meeting of the new black assembly.

---

[19] Fanon, "Antillais et Africain," *op. cit.* p. 265.
[20] Quoted in *Time*, April 6, 1970, p. 23.

"Political action is based on self-interest. It happens that in this instance that self-interest is based on race."[21]

Above all, the most positive and vital legacy of Césaire's négritude is the theme of black pride. In Washington, a private organization established to create jobs for black youth and build up black business is significantly called "Pride, Inc." Black consciousness is expressed in practical terms in the universities, with insistence on black studies programs and with the start of black studies groups in various youth organizations. Before he died, the Urban League's Whitney Young summarized a new measure of black pride by suggesting that black strengths are an asset to be exchanged with white America, rather than absorbed by it. The slogan "Black is beautiful!" is 100 percent négritude.

Finally, just as Césaire's preoccupation with négritude precluded his involvement with other trends in the thirties, the black cause is the principle, and sometimes only, focus of black activists. It was no accident that during the anti-pollution demonstrations of the sixties, the black community was conspicuous by its absence. Again, during the anti-Vietnam war demonstrations on American campuses, black power groups took no significant part.

Going one step further, some black leaders now even suggest that what is good for the black community is best for America. At the close of the 1972 black convention, one D.C. delegate said,

> We lift up a black agenda recognizing that white America moves toward the abyss created by its own racist arrogance, misplaced priorities, rampant materialism and ethical bankruptcy. Therefore, we are certain that the agenda we now press for . . . is not only for the future of black humanity, but is probably the only way the rest of America can save itself from the harvest of its criminal past.[22]

Although his literary work is probably read by only a few of the more educated leaders in the black world, the essence of Césaire's négritude, whether consciously adopted or not, is not only the guts of modern black culture, but is also a major ingredient in the political and social development of the entire black community.

"Négritude was an historic stage, a point of departure," says Césaire quite simply. "It played its role in the awakening of the black world . . . the blacks of the world make up a kind of community, ideas circulate within that community . . . there are repercussions everywhere."[23]

---

[21] Quoted in the *Washington Post,* March 13, 1972, p. 1.
[22] D.C. Del. Walter Fauntroy, quoted in the *Washington Post,* March 13, 1972, p. 8.
[23] My interview.

IV
COMMUNISM — An Uneasy Experiment

Once home in Martinique, Césaire focused his attention on revitalizing Antillean culture and awakening the blacks of Martinique to the full implications of the négritude ideology he was formulating. He founded a local review called *Tropique,* in which he broke with the tradition of assimilation: he described Martiniquais society as it was; he celebrated Antillean folklore and rejected all imitative literature; he retraced the blacks' African origins and heritage, including the black slave trade; most important, he extolled the virtues of being black and offered hope for freedom from the legacy of slavery. In short, Césaire wrote of things which no black Martiniquais had wished to think or remember, much less address openly: he articulated the island's social malaise for the first time. "The fact of simply affirming that one is black, as I affirmed it, was a revolutionary postulate,"[1] declared Césaire in later years. His revolutionary ideas struck a responsive chord in Martinique both amongst the aggressive intellectuals and the disaffected masses. His popularity and influence surged. Since the exigencies of the new consciousness which Césaire inspired in the black community inevitably demanded changes in the political and social life of the island, it is not surprising that Césaire emerged in 1945 as a political figure—and that the electorate overwhelmingly voted him deputy to the National Assembly and mayor of Fort-de-France. What was a little surprising was that Césaire was the standard-bearer of the Communist Party of Martinique, under whose banner he retained his two offices for the next ten years, following the Party line as handed down by the French Communist Party.

There is nothing to indicate Césaire's political affiliations before 1945, certainly not his *Notebook on Returning Home,* which we must accept as the expression of his deepest feelings at that time. In fact, Césaire's commitment to the Communist Party seemed to be in direct contradiction to his previous attitudes. For underlying this new affiliation was an implied return to the European sphere of influence, his commitment to a movement founded on European ideology and his unequivocal support of "departmentalization," which presupposed the closest possible ties between the island and France.

Césaire recounts that, in fact, his leadership of the Communist Party of Martinique came about quite by chance: "It was an adventure. I was not at all predisposed to [a political career] but it took the delirium of the Liberation: one starts from scratch and does almost anything . . . And, for my part,

---

[1]Césaire, Quoted in "Un Poète Politique: Aimé Césaire:" *Magazine Littéraire, op. cit.,* p. 29. (My translation.)

it was a gesture of solidarity with a certain number of people who had had confidence in me. I had convictions, which are absolutely those which I have now, Marxist convictions—or Marxist-leaning—but that did not imply, in my opinion, the launching of a political career."[2] This is certainly consistent with the postwar atmosphere, not only in Martinique, but throughout the West Indies, where intellectuals like Césaire, Jacques Romain, Nicolás Guillén and countless others who embraced négritude and sympathized with Marxism now became active communists. For those intellectuals who were looking for answers to the perennial problems of colonial exploitation, the events of the war years in the Antilles undoubtedly heightened the appeal of the communist doctrines of racial equality and anti-colonialism and the identification of all evils with capitalism and imperialism. The white metropolitan proletarians, victims of bourgeois capitalist exploitation, seemed their natural allies.

> They . . . felt that the problem of their countrymen's emancipation reaches beyond the limited confines of the Caribbean archipelago, that it is inseparably wedded to a universal problem, and that therefore it requires to be integrated into a universal cause. And that is why they joined not only in the battle waged by the world's Negroes against racial prejudice, but also and above all in that struggle where all the downtrodden people of this earth, regardless of their race or colour, are participants against the capitalist regime.[3]

For practical purposes, the Communist Party of Martinique, as an arm of the French Communist Party, offered badly-needed support and experience as well as a vehicle to national political power for these new political leaders. This was of considerable importance for those who believed that solutions to the islands' problems might come from above, from a government which had the interests of the working class and possibly the black colonials at heart. In addition, achieving their goals within the framework of the French government had the advantage of providing the islands with protection against the possibility of a real or imagined threat from the "white dog of the North,"[4] the United States. Some, if not all of these considerations undoubtedly played a role in Césaire's decision to lead the Communist Party to the polls right after the war.

Martinique's local elections of 1945 were, characteristically, a left-wing landslide: two out of three deputies to the National Assembly (one being Aimé Césaire) and the new mayor of Fort-de-France (Aimé Césaire), ran on the Communist Party ticket, while of the thirty-six members of the Conseil Général, fourteen were communists, twelve were socialists.[5] The postwar trend

---

[2]*Ibid.*

[3]Guérin, *The West Indies And Their Future, op. cit.,* p. 107.

[4]Césaire, *Cahier D'Un Retour Au Pays Natal, op. cit.,* p. 89.

[5]Guérin, *The West Indies and Their Future, op. cit.,* p. 113.

of the intellectual leaders toward extreme left positions also had occurred in the general electorate, but for slightly different reasons. Aimé Césaire bridged the gap.

As far as the Martiniquais populace was concerned, the vote in 1945 was certainly in part a protest against white sugar planters and "the fundamental treason of a large section of the established Church and State"[6] during the war. This resulted in a split in the relatively conservative Radical Socialist Party, allowing the Communist Party to capture the vote. In addition, the practice of sending elected deputies to Paris had always had the effect of duplicating the political cross-currents of Europe in the overseas departments and setting up ties with the French parties. Therefore, when the communists and socialists came to participate in power in France, after the war, it was only natural that the departments reflect the trend. Thirdly, the Latin American and Caribbean penchant for loyalty to a 'strong leader might have been a factor. If in 1939 the Communist Party of Martinique could count on 100-200 votes and by 1944 the Party had gained so rapidly that it was the only effective mass organization in the political field, it was due at least in part to the enormous personal influence of Aimé Césaire. His négritude was by then well-known, and it was the touchstone of the new popular movement, the essence behind Daniel Guérin's observation that:

> Racial consciousness . . . *colours,* if one may permit oneself the word, the . . . rather abstract concept of class-struggle by injecting something palpable into it, something the islanders can see and feel . . . the islander was prone to feel far more resentful over insults directed at his race than over the economic iniquities to which he was subjected. It is not so much the prospects of socialism and communism, but the revolt against racial persecution that has stirred the grandchildren of slaves from their secular passivity.[7]

During the decade of his leadership of the Communist Party of Martinique, by far the most consuming political question for Martinique revolved around her departmentalization. Césaire's record on that matter is directly related to his position vis-à-vis the Communist Party and lends a great deal of insight into his quality as a communist.

In 1945 the Communist Party of Martinique advocated the island's amalgamation into the French Republic. This was a reflection of the policy dictated by the strongly centrist French Communist Party, for whom the creation of another communist-oriented department had the practical appeal of increasing their parliamentary strength. In the debates before the vote on the law of 1946, Césaire strenuously supported the program for departmentalization. Departmentalization represented a definitive step toward the ending of Mar-

---

[6]Blanshard, *Democracy and Empire in the Caribbean, op. cit.,* p. 253.
[7]Guérin, *The West Indies and Their Future, op. cit.,* p. 104.

tinique's status as a colony, he argued. Integration into France was the logical conclusion of the historical and cultural process which

> has tended to eliminate all important differences of mores and civiliza-
> tion between the people of France and those of these territories,
> and to make it so that their future can only be conceived of in the
> constantly narrower incorporation into the metropolitan life.[8]

The territories had the right, said Césaire, to a status that would guarantee them the rights and laws of France. Complete assimilation of the old colonies into the metropole would thus be the best response to the racists. And, he added, it would prove "a new guarantee for these territories against foreign encroachment."[9]

It was partly due to Césaire's unequivocal and vigorous support that the vote on the law of 1946 in Martinique was overwhelmingly for departmentalization.

By 1956, however, Aimé Césaire emerged as one of the foremost critics of departmentalization, which he then renounced as reactionary and contradictory.

Clearly, there was wide-spread disappointment in the results of the application of French laws to the former colony. Martinique's welfare hadn't improved through its new status. While the administrative machinery of the island had been completely upset, the hoped-for dynamic development of the economy and reform of the social structure had not materialized. (see Chapter II.)

It was Césaire's conviction that this was due to departmentalization's assimilationist character, which remained inherently colonial. If the rigorous application of France's laws to the islands redressed one previously invidious condition, at the same time it created a new one, for French policies retained the stigma and the essence of abhorrent colonialism. The Antilles should have the right of self-determination, concluded Césaire.

This denunciation of departmentalization was indicative not only of Césaire's reversion to an earlier overt anti-European, anti-assimilationist stance, but significantly, of his increasing personal dissatisfaction within the Communist Party. For, in attacking departmentalization, he was simultaneously refuting the French Communist Party line and coincidentally his own Communist Party of Martinique.

> Rather early, I had the impression that the communists were also
> assimilationists. Within the Communist Party I found that I was just
> like a colonial . . . the Martiniquais party wasn't even a party, it
> was a section of the French Communist Party: the decisions were
> made in Paris and we were expected to apply them. . . I asked the

---

[8]Victor Sablé, *La Transformation des Îles D'Amérique en Départements Français*, (Paris: Larose, 1955.) p. 146. (My translation).
[9]*Ibid.*, p. 146.

Martiniquais federation to transform itself into a Martiniquais party, to have a political line based on Martiniquais nationalism—these ideas were fought by my comrades who wanted to remain loyal to the French apparatus.[10]

Césaire had in effect discovered the same thing that Senghor realized with regard to Africa: all parties, even those on the Left, which were protegés of French national parties, were at the same time "pawns on the chessboard of the French parliamentary game . . . national parties, formed by national realities and oriented toward national interests. And . . . the French proletariat indirectly benefitted from colonial exploitation."[11]

If the question of departmentalization reveals Césaire's inability to come to grips with the European-oriented Communist Party organization, careful examination of his literary work during these dozen or so years yields abundant evidence that from the start Césaire's commitment to communism as a philosophy was on all levels ambiguous and constantly compromised by his commitment to négritude.

Between 1939 and 1955, precisely the years of his leadership of the Communist Party of Martinique, Césaire's literary output was confined to poetry which is simply the development of the main theses of *Notebook on Returning Home*. Contained in two anthologies—*Les Armes Miraculeuses* (1946) and *Soleil Cou Coupé* (1948)—these poems stand out in stark contrast to the writings of other communist poets at the time. For example, Louis Aragón, the French poet, wrote for and of the French Resistance movement. Nicolás Guillén, the Cuban communist,. reflected the burning issues of the day with such diverse titles as "Soldados en Abisinia," "Tres canciones chinas," "La pequeña balada de Plovdiv (Bulgaria)." Pablo Neruda, the Chilean communist, also created odes to local Communist Party leaders such as "Prestes del Brasil" and "Recabarren" and rhapsodized the glories of the Soviet Union with "Nuevo canto de amor a Stalingrado" and "Canto al ejército rojo a su llegada a los puertos de Rusia." Césaire, however, never even contributed to the clandestine literary propaganda organ *Les Cahiers de la Libération*.[12] His preoccupations were of an entirely different nature, if his poetry of the time is any indication of them. *Les Armes Miraculeuses* and *Le Soleil Cou Coupé* contain odes almost exclusively concerned with African, Negro, primitive and nature-oriented themes: "Le Pur-Sang," "Tam-Tam De Nuit," "Conquête De L'Aube" *(Les Armes Miraculeuses)*, "Mississipi," [sic.] "À L'Afrique," "Ode á La Guinée" *(Le Soleil Cou Coupé)*, etc.

---

[10]Césaire, quoted in *Magazine Littéraire, op. cit.*, p. 29. (My translation.)

[11]Léopold Sédar Senghor, *On African Socialism*, (New York: Praeger, 1964.) p. 3.

[12]*Les Cahiers de la Liberation* was published in 1943-1945 in Martinique, Guadeloupe and Guyana. Césaire did contribute at this time to *Martinique*, a purely literary review.

Demonstrating the bent of Césaire's thoughts even more conclusively is the "poem-play" *Et Les Chiens Se Taisaient* . . . which completes *Les Armes Miraculeuses.* The Rebel, a slave, symbolized the poet, a Christ of his people, who has killed his white planter-master and is condemned to death. His sacrifice is the symbol of the revolt of his fallen race, of a bleeding Africa, of all tortured peoples and their leaders who grasp for self-understanding. The Architect, in turn, represented the blue-eyed white man who is warned in terms reminiscent of *Notebook on Returning Home:*

> be careful Architect for if the Rebel dies it will not be without having made clear to everyone that you are the builder of a world of pestilence . . .[13]

Césaire wrote this rather violent tragedy in 1943—during the Vichy occupation of Martinique and in the year of the Battle of Stalingrad and the Allied landings in Italy. He was still preoccupied with the plight of the oppressed, enslaved blacks of the island, he identified with their cause, and he hoped for their future.

In short, these two anthologies represent a continuation or development of the motifs of *Notebook on Returning Home* and ignore, to no less a degree than it did in the thirties, the mainstream of communist thought in the forties.

If Césaire's poetry in the forties is obscure, flamboyant, emotional and revealing by omission, his political writing of the fifties is lucid, articulate, emotional, and revealing by its content. The first such paper that we have is his *Discourse on Colonialism,* published in 1955. In this work, he defines the destructive relationship between European civilization and colonization, further identifies the Africa whose heritage he had accepted in *Notebook on Returning Home,* and declares that Europe has created two major problems: 1) the problem of the proletariat and 2) the colonial problem.

Analyzing the realities of European civilization, Césaire, in the *Discourse,* writes that it is moribund and indefensible; its judges are millions of enslaved victims of its colonization throughout the world who are now aware of its basic hypocrisy. The "Big Lie" that Europe has perpetrated throughout two hundred years of colonization is the same lie that Césaire decried in *Notebook on Returning Home.* The truth of the matter lies in seeing European colonization as it really is—starting with what it is not:

> neither evangelization, nor philanthropic undertaking, nor the desire to push back the frontiers of ignorance, disease or tyranny, nor the spread of religion, nor the extension of the rule of *Law;* . . . the decisive action is that of the adventurer, the pirate, of the wholesale grocers and ship owners, of the gold seekers and merchants, of greed and force behind which lurks the malevolent shadow, of a form of civilization which at a certain moment in its history finds itself com-

---

[13] Aimé Césaire, *Les Armes Miraculeuses* (Paris: Gillimard, 1946.), p. 97. (My translation).

pelled by internal reasons to extend to the entire world the competition of its antagonistic economies.

. . . .

. . . Between *colonization* and *civilization* the distance is infinite; . . . from all the colonial expeditions, from all the elaborate colonial statutes, from all the ministerial circulars sent out, not a single human value was gained.[14]

According to Césaire, colonization, by definition, negates civilization; it is founded on contempt for indigenous people, turning them into an "instrument of production." *"Colonisation = dehumanization"* says Césaire. "They talk about civilization, I call it proletarianization and mystification."[15] European so-called civilization, itself, by accepting the degrading, immoral, violent, racist colonization has become dehumanized and decivilized, poisoned by its own hypocrisy and pseudo-humanism, inevitably giving birth to Nazism, for which it was an accomplice before becoming the victim. Elaborating on this argument, Césaire accounts for his complete contempt of Europe and his astonishing disregard of the entire anti-fascist struggle in the late thirties:

> Yes, it would be worthwhile to study clinically, in detail, the proceedings of Hitler and hitlerism and to reveal to the very distinguished, very humanist, very Christian bourgeois of the 20th century, that without knowing he carries a Hitler within himself, that Hitler *lives* inside him, that Hitler is his *demon,* that if he denounces him, it is illogical, and that underneath it all what he cannot pardon in Hitler is not *the crime* in itself, *the crime against man,* it is not *the humiliation of man in itself,* it is the crime against the white man, it is the humiliation of the white man, and of having applied to Europe the colonialist procedures which until now have only been experienced by the Algerian Arabs, the Indian coolies, and the African Negroes.
>
> . . . .
>
> The logical conclusion of capitalism hoping to perpetuate itself is Hitler. The logical conclusion of formal humanism and philosophical renunciation is Hitler.[16]

Césaire regards Nazism as just another manifestation of the racism of the entire white civilization; the "most horrendous white racism of all" being European colonialism, the exigencies of which define and widen the gulf between the humanistic ideals preached by Europeans and the unprincipled realities of their behavior. Césaire's obsession and identification with the oppression of black men patently preclude his empathizing with white Europeans victimized by a racism of which they themselves are fundamentally guilty. Nevertheless, Césaire protests once more that he is neither an enemy of Europe nor a prophet of a return to an ante-European past. He does not

---

[14] Aimé Césaire, *Discours Sur Le Colonialisme,* 3rd edition, revised and augmented (Paris: Présence Africaine, 1955.),pp. 9-10. (All quotes from this work are my translation.)

[15] *Ibid.,* pp. 21-23.

[16] *Ibid.,* pp. 12-13.

deny the importance of Europe in the history of human thought. But he regrets the old societies, destroyed by imperialism, which he maintains, were communal, anti- as well as ante-capitalist, democratic, cooperative, and fraternal. He rues the fate of Africa which, coming into contact with the rest of the world too late, had the misfortune of meeting head-on a Europe which had already fallen into the clutches of unscrupulous financiers and captains of industry who propagated feudal injustices. In short, "Colonial Europe has heaped modern abuse upon ancient injustice; odious racism on the old inequality."[17] And the violence, racism, and immorality of the bourgeois class which perpetuates them only signify that that class is fighting its approaching demise.

Now, the past must be surpassed, wrote Césaire, and the present replaced:

> With the help of all our enslaved brothers we must create a new society rich with all the modern productive power, warm with all the antique fraternity. The Soviet Union gives us a few examples that show this is possible.[18]

Here is Césaire's only reference to the Soviet Union, and, at that, he doesn't elaborate to define its example.

The new society, which will be Europe's salvation, if she takes the initiative, must be based on two things: nationalities and revolution toward a classless society.

> . . . if Western Europe does not take, herself . . . at the threshold of South Africa . . . at the gates of America, the initiative of a policy of *nationalities,* the initiative of a new policy founded on the respect of peoples and cultures; what can I say? If Europe neither galvanizes moribund cultures nor gives birth to new ones; if she does not awaken other nations and civilizations. . . . Europe will have deprived herself of her ultimate *chance* . . . the salvation of Europe will not be achieved by a revolution in methods; it will result from the *Revolution*: that which will substitute for the narrow tyranny of a dehumanized bourgeoisie, while awaiting the classless society, the preponderance of the only class which still has a universal mission, for it embodies the suffering of all the evils of history, all the universal evils: the proletariat.[19]

These last two paragraphs illustrate Césaire's attempt to reconcile his deepest feelings with Marxism. His approach is Marxist and he finally proclaims the proletariat the standard-bearer of the Revolution. But he does not succeed in relating this to his prime concern, and throughout the *Discourse,* Césaire's emphasis remains on the primacy of racial problems—and preoccupation with race is incompatible with Marxism. In the *Discourse,* more than in any of his other writings he describes the colonial peoples' struggle in terms of the

---

[17]*Ibid.,* pp. 24-26.
[18]*Ibid.,* pp. 34-35.
[19]*Ibid.,* pp. 70-71.

universal revolt of the proletariat; but it is almost as though he has to remind himself that the white world he is denouncing is the white bourgeoisie, and the oppressed and exploited colored peoples are one with the white workers suffering under the same system. Hubert Juin, in a profile of Césaire, puts it another way:

> . . . he wants to go from the particular to the universal, but he tries to renounce neither of them. He wants to remain the Negro that he is, that he is proud to be. But he wants also to achieve a world in which we two, Black and White, will live as neighbors and exchange the best that we each have and especially that which is measured only by quality and not quantity. The equality of man is a theorem which permits thinking that the Europeanization . . . of conquered continents is possible by methods other than occupation and the race for dividends.[20]

Ultimately, however, Césaire's universalism is conditional; his preeminent concern is consistently with the fate of the Negro race and indigenous cultures oppressed by colonialism. At the First International Congress of Negro Writers and Artists in September, 1956, Césaire reaffirms this prejudice; it is particularly notable when compared with statements made by other blacks at the Congress.

The Congress was inspired and organized by a Negro literary review, *Présence Africaine,* dedicated to reaffirming Negro culture. It convened in Paris, attracting black intellectuals from all over the world to discuss and exchange ideas on the theme: "The Crisis of Negro Culture." The papers presented centered mainly around the nature of Negro culture, if indeed there was one, and its relationship to Western civilization. From the outset, there was a divergence of opinion between the English-speaking and the French-speaking blacks. Representative of the former, the New World group, was Richard Wright who approached the question with what he called "double-vision": that of a black man who is the product of Western civilization. He is able, therefore, to see and understand both points of view from another, third, point of view, without negating his racial identity or becoming an enemy of the West.[21]

John A. Davis identified even more strongly with the Western civilization of which he is a member: He presented himself as an American Negro, fundamentally opposed to colonialism, but in search of pragmatic solutions and a realistic approach to post-colonialism. A bloodless change must be made, he said, in terms of democratic ideas and within the institutions which are part of the culture to which the black man belongs. As a minority in the

---

[20] Hubert Juin, *Aimé Césaire* (Paris: Présence Africaine, 1956.), pp. 77-78.
[21] Richard Wright, "Tradition and Industrialization," *Présence Africaine, Le 1er Congrès International des Ecrivains et Artistes Noirs,* No. spécial, 19-22 Septembre 1956, Paris, p. 349.

country, he concluded, the American Negro is looking forward to a complete, equal status as citizen, not to any self-determination.[22]

The British West African, Davidson Nicol, presented another interesting attitude toward the relationship between Negro culture and Western civilization: The nineteenth century attitude of easy social interracial mixing and a policy which leads to self-government, he said, counteracts extreme nationalism, communism, and racial bitterness. The motive power is thus lacking to stimulate Afro-European conflict.[23]

The antithesis of these attitudes was presented by Aimé Césaire— "undoubtedly the dominating figure" at the Congress, according to several observers.[24] In his paper, "Culture and Colonization," Césaire told the delegates that the common denominator of their diversified group was "the colonial situation" and, whether one wishes or not, the problem of black culture goes hand in hand with the problem of colonialism.[25] It follows from this that the problems of a Negro culture are directly dependent upon the stage or degree of colonization under which it is developing: the degree of cultural development is inversely proportionate to the degree of political suppression

> . . . a political and social regime which suppresses the self-determination of a people kills at the same time the creative power of the people . . . where there has been colonization, entire nations have been drained of their culture, drained of all culture . . . the ability to *excel* is in all living civilization and every civilization is living when the society in which it is expressed is free.[26]

Defining a civilization as the coordinated whole of social, technical, intellectual, and organizational functions, Césaire contended that a colonizer cannot transfer his civilization to the colony for it would mean nothing less than the building up of an indigenous capitalist society, which, as a reflection of the metropolitan, is at the same time, by definition, its competitor.[27] The logic of the colonizer in its relationship with the colony is to retain all control of political, military and economic organization through the process of strict selectivity. Following this line of thought, Césaire rejected the possibility of "une civilisation métisse" resulting from the give and take between an indigenous civilization and a colonial civilization. He believed a synthesized civiliza-

---

[22]John Davis, in "Debates," *Présence Africaine, Le 1er Congrès International. Ecrivains et Artistes Noirs,* No. spécial, 19-22 Septembre 1956, Paris, pp. 214-215.

[23]Davidson Nicol, "The Soft Pink Palms," *Présence Africaine, Le 1er Congrès International des Écrivains et Artistes Noirs,* No. spécial, 19-22 Septembre 1956, Paris, p. 121.

[24]Colin Legum, *Pan Africanism* (New York: Frederick A. Praeger, 1965.), p. 98. Also see a very interesting account of the conference and Césaire in James Baldwin, *Nobody Knows My Name* (New York: Dell, 1961.), Chapter 2.

[25]Aimé Césaire "Culture et Colonisation," *Présence Africaine, Le 1er Congrès International des Ecrivains et Artistes Noirs,* No. spécial, 19-22 Septembre 1956, Paris, p. 190. (My translation.)

[26]*Ibid.,* p. 194.

[27]*Ibid.,* p. 198.

tion could be valid only if the transfer of civilization corresponded to the exigencies of the internal situation and could thus lead to assimilation by integration, not imposition.[28]

The situation in the colonial countries today, concluded Césaire, is one of juxtaposed, rather than harmonized, cultural traits. The imposition of foreign cultures on indigenous civilizations has created a cultural anarchy. The solution is to liberate colonial people so that they might synthesize their indigenous cultural traits and those elements they wish to borrow from Europe. In so doing, they would surpass both old (i.e., African) culures and new (i.e., European).

Césaire's speech aroused great enthusiasm from the crowded hall, but it also engendered the wrath of the Americans present, who could see no connection between the question of colonization and their participation in a Congress called to discuss the problems of Negro culture. Césaire insisted that all Negroes were currently suffering from the direct effects of colonization or the racist sequel to slavery (e.g., in the United States). It was the response of the African and close friend of Césaire, Léopold Sédar Senghor, that best defined Césaire's own position and at the same time revealed his difficulty in coming to terms with communism. Speaking just after Davis in the debate that followed Césaire's paper, Senghor said:

> We wish, therefore, to liberate ourselves politically to be able in effect to express our négritude, that is to say, our true black values.
> But when we will have obtained what you [Americans] call equality, and what we call 'the defeat of colonialism' . . . another question will be raised, that was raised the other day by Wright . . . Being American, is he the heir of European civilization, or African civilization, or American civilization? But Césaire and I have often asked ourselves this question.
> Many of us are Marxists. But Marx was not an African. His doctrine was born out of man's situation in Western Europe. And he himself said that this theory in *Capital* was only valid for Western Europe. Therefore, we too, we are, objectively, mixed breeds—and it is on this point that I will 'argue' with Césaire, while agreeing with him. Today, we are, objectively, cultural hybrids . . .
>
> . . . .
>
> But Césaire is right when he says that . . . one must not be assimilated; one must assimilate . . . The problem, for us, consists first of all in ridding ourselves of this political alienation. Césaire did not propose any solutions for us. He did not say to us: 'It is the communist solution, it is the socialist solution, it is the democratic solution, etc.' . . .[29]

Senghor put his finger on the contradiction with which Césaire was faced. For Césaire, like Wright, had double vision: he considered himself a Marxist

---

[28]*Ibid.,* p. 200.
[29]Léopold Senghor, in "Debates," *Présence Africaine, Le 1er Congrès International des Ecrivains et Artistes Noirs,* No. spécial, 19-22 septembre 1956. Paris. pp. 215-216. (My translation.)

revolutionary, but because of his strong identification with négritude, Marxism could only be valid to the degree that it was applicable to the colonial situation and its defeat; from that point on, his négritude dictated a commitment to specifically Negro values, not Negro values assimilated by a European or Western civilization. Furthermore, Césaire's deep-seated hatred of the white world prevented his acceptance, once colonialism was defeated, of solutions based on European assumptions. Post-colonialist solutions must be tailored along national political and cultural lines.

This line of reasoning was incorporated into Césaire's attitude toward departmentalization, which, as we have seen, had come full circle between 1946 and 1956. In his introduction to Daniel Guérin's book, *Les Antilles Décolonisées,* Césaire focused on the contradictions inherent in and created by departmentalization and proposed a "national solution":

> . . . for the Antillean peoples, progress will consist, as for the other colonial peoples, of passing from absorption in the dismal universality of an empire, to the participation in the living spirit of nations that have finally achieved individuality.
>
> That is what took me so long to realize.
>
> That, and also the idea that there are two ways of looking at the French Antilles: one is to declare regretfully that of the dependent regions of the world they are among the slowest and most hesitating to accept the idea of nationality; the other by considering the Antilles the most typically revealing case of all the unfortunate experiences through which all colonial peoples pass before ending up at *the inevitable awakening of their national conscience.*
>
> . . . as is well known, nationalist demands have developed out of demands that were apparently assimilationist.
>
> . . . it is inevitable that Antillean assimilationism will be superceded
>
> . . . Ten years after the law which transformed the French Antilles into French departments, each of these Antilles by the deceptions and pauses of the present, has come to the idea of nationality and it is on this reality alone that it will be possible from now on to build the future.[30]

Taking issue with Guérin's discussion of postwar changes in the Antilles, Césaire accused Guérin of having failed to recognize the development of national consciousness along with the rise of racial and social consciousness. The "particularism" of each Antillean country represents an embryonic culture, a valid national community, Césaire contended. Predicting objections to his following this line of reasoning to its logical conclusion, in which each little island would become a nation unto itself, Césaire countered:

> There is no 'slight nationality.' If the mediation for liberty is always done by nation, the scantiest of nationalities will always be infinitely more substantial than the richest of imperial abstractions.
>
> . . . tossed about between two human families which confront him

---

[30] Guérin, *Les Antilles Décolonisées,* with introduction by Césaire, pp. 12-14. (My translation.)

with a double disregard, the Antillean will only have a chancè to extricate himself *in establishing his own original family.*[31]

Césaire even rejected as visionary the idea of an Antillean federation, based either on an enlargement of the British West Indies Federation or on a new Caribbean concept: a more viable and coherent solution would be that the Antilles, after having reached national maturity, will freely decide to unite for mutual benefit in a confederation or "regional group."[32]

By 1956, therefore, both his literary work and his political activity reveal that Césaire failed to reconcile his fundamental beliefs with the communism he outwardly supported. His declared adherence to Marxism could only have been conditional. Césaire's consistent obsession with race was aptly illustrated in the *Discourse on Colonialism* and his paper "Culture and Colonization." Furthermore, his open espousal of Martiniquais nationalism reflects not only disappointment with departmentalization, but also disillusionment with the Communist Party. For Césaire, neither European solutions nor affiliations with European parties were acceptable in 1956.

Césaire's letter of resignation from the Communist Party in October of that year should have surprised no one who knew him or his writings well: they were moving inexorably in that direction. But the circumstances surrounding the letter and its intellectual arguments repudiating communism render it a unique, if not sensational, document.

---

[31]*Ibid.*, pp. 15-16.
[32]*Ibid.*, p. 17.

V

RESIGNATION — An Independent Course

In the wake of destalinization, the only communist leader who took the definitive stand of publicly resigning in protest against what the party had stood for all the preceding years was Aimé Césaire, a Caribbean black. Césaire's letter of resignation from the French Communist Party, coming as it did during the fever of late Fall 1956, has almost universally been considered a direct result of the Hungarian Revolution, or at the very least, of the effects of destalinization. As a matter of fact, Césaire's letter was signed October 24, 1956, almost simultaneously with the Hungarian uprising; but it was certainly conceived, if not written, before that date, and there is, in any case, no mention at all of the events in Hungary. What is more than likely is that the shock waves sent out by the Twentieth Congress of the Communist Party of the Soviet Union created the atmosphere, and the Polish uprising of Fall 1956, provided the trigger for Césaire's action: careful analysis of the context in which the letter was written as well as the letter itself, reveals it as a watershed in his career, a unique synthesis of all those views intrinsic to Césaire's philosophy.

In a secret report to the Twentieth Congress of the Communist Party of the Soviet Union on February 25, 1956, Khrushchev disclosed the horrendous crimes Stalin had perpetrated against the Soviet people in the name of Socialism and through his "personality cult." In destroying Stalin's revered image, Khrushchev unleashed a wave of "destalinization" throughout the communist world—a reappraisal of Stalin's policies and renunciation of Stalinist methods. The text of the speech began to "leak out" by March 18-19, 1956, and was published, in full, in France, June 6, 1956.[1]

Under the leadership of Maurice Thorez, the French Communist Party (which had always been one of the most faithful Stalinist parties), reacted cautiously. Stalin's errors could take nothing away from his contributions, said Thorez: it was a matter of putting everything into perspective. The Communist Party line was right and Stalin's errors could not change that. What was wrong, according to Thorez, was simply the personality cult.[2] The Fourteenth Party Congress of the French Communist Party met at Le Havre July 18-July 21, 1956. A few intellectuals dissented from the general line (which was to minimize the impact of destalinization), but Thorez had the situation well in hand. He proclaimed continued solidarity with the Communist Party of the Soviet Union and criticized those who demanded that the French Communist Party engage in self-criticism, on the grounds that the party was not

[1]*Le Monde*, June 6, 1956, pp. 2-3.
[2]*Le Monde*, March 28, 1956, p. 4, col. 1; April 21, 1956, p. 6, col. 1.

a debate club nor had it been guilty of Stalinist methods. In spite of Thorez's denial of the charge that intellectuals were ordered to a passive obedience in the French Communist Party, many had already been dismissed from the review *Economie et Politique* and the newspaper *Humanité* when they had taken "destalinization" literally to mean an opportunity to air their opinions.[3] In addition, Thorez defended the March 14 party vote in the French National Assembly on Algeria, in which 132 out of 144 communists—including Aimé Césaire![4]—voted confidence in the government and gave it special powers to deal with the Algerian revolt. This communist stand was justified by Thorez as a desire for a broad front with the socialist workers, i.e., rapprochement with the socialist parties in the government.[5] But it clearly implied power for the Guy Mollet government to call up reserves and increase the strength of French armed forces in Algeria.

While the French Communist Party was busy saving face, other parties in Eastern Europe and in Italy were showing signs of liberalization, or at least ferment. In the midst of all this, the First International Congress of Negro Writers and Artists (discussed at length in Chapter IV) convened. This unique gathering was intellectually and culturally stimulating to Aimé Césaire's fecund imagination. Just one month later, Césaire's letter to Thorez was published.

At the outset, Césaire levelled his attack against both International Communism, under the hegemony of the Soviet Union, and the French Communist Party and cited Khrushchev's disclosures about the Stalin era as a "record-breaking crop" of grievances against them. Furthermore, continued Césaire, in the wake of Khrushchev's revelations about the true nature of Stalinist-type communist parties, the attitude of the French Communist Party at their Fourteenth Congress unequivocally exposed that Party's "glaring deficiencies." Césaire roundly denounced the French Communist Party for its

> conspicuous lack of haste to seize the offered opportunity and to declare their independence of Russia . . . reluctance to get going in the direction of destalinization . . . its unwillingness to condemn Stalin and the methods that led him to crime . . . its unassailable self-satisfaction . . . antidemocratic methods dear to Stalin . . . pigheaded obstinateness in error; perseverance in lies; the fantastic pretense of never once having been wrong . . . a senile incapacity to rise from their own routine confines to the level of events . . . in the middle of the general storm, the French Party gazes fondly into the mirror and announces that it's satisfied . . .[6]

---

[3]*Le Monde,* July 18, 1956, p. 5, col. 2.

[4]*Le Monde,* March 14, 1956, p. 5, col. 3.

[5]*Le Monde,* July 19, 1956, p. 16, col. 2. Or read Etienne Fajon, "La Lutte Pour La Paix en Algérie." Paris, 1956. p. 13.

[6]Aimé Césaire, "Letter to Maurice Thorez" (Paris: Présence Africaine, 1957.) pp. 4-6.

But this embittered diatribe hurled against the French Communist Party for its current complacency had been building up in Césaire during his decade of experience in its ranks.

Looking back on his resignation, Césaire explains that he bitterly resented the fact that the Communist Party of Martinique was considered only a section of and, therefore, subordinate to the French Communist Party. As such he was slavishly committed to following a line set down in Paris, and more often than not, in Moscow.

"I am against the official party line," said Césaire recently. "It is a moral question . . . I don't like being regimented in a party which isn't my own."[7]

Even more pertinent, perhaps, was the personal alienation which Césaire felt within the Party. For, however indicative the recent events were of the "bankruptcy of an ideal and pathetic illustration of a whole generation's failure," the determining factor for Césaire's appraisal lay in "considerations which have to do with my condition and quality of a colored man."[8] The following passage is self-explanatory:

> I have acquired the conviction that our ways and destinies, and those of communism, such as it is put into practice, are not purely and simply identical; that they cannot be purely and simply identified . . .
> We colored men, have consciously grasped and grasped in its full breadth the notion of our peculiar uniqueness . . . The peculiarity of 'our place in the world' . . . the peculiarity of our problems, which aren't to be reduced subordinated forms of any other problems . . . the peculiarity of our history . . . the peculiarity of our culture.[9]

These specifically black considerations are simply the several parts of what Césaire sums up as "the colonial question"—and it is in its solutions to this all-important problem that communism has manifestly failed for Césaire. Alluding to the recent French Communist Party vote on Algeria, in which Césaire's participation was apparently a source of self-recrimination, he laid bare the heart of the matter:

> . . . the colonial question, cannot be treated as a subsidiary part of some more important global matter, as a part over which deals can be arranged or upon which others can patch up compromises they think they have a right to seek in the name of an overall situation which they retain the exclusive right to interpret . . . our colonialism, the struggle of coloured peoples against racism, is much more complex, indeed, it is of a totally different nature than the struggle of the French workers against French capitalism, and cannot in any case be considered as a part, as a fragment, of that struggle.[10]

Nothing could more clearly illustrate the irreconcilable incompatibility, the

---

[7]My interview.
[8]Césaire, "Letter to Maurice Thorez", *op cit*. p. 6.
[9]*Ibid.*, pp. 6-7.
[10]*Ibid.*, p. 7.

fundamental contradiction, between the cause to which Césaire was—and is—committed, by philosophy and by nature, and communism.

But Césaire had other grievances which grew out of the specifics of his political frame of reference. Being from a rural, peasant society, where the working class is small and the middle class exercises political power out of proportion to their numerical strength, he questioned whether a communist organization can achieve concrete results "in the name of an exclusive ideology rejecting *a priori* basically decent and profoundly anti-colonialist men."[11] This exclusivity reflected the European political realities, perhaps, but not those of an island like Martinique. And, in addition, the Communist Party of Martinique, like those in other colonialist countries, was "federated with or enfeoffed to the metropolitan . . . party"[12] and, therefore, was denied the effective handling of its own affairs.

> There is a great wind of unity soughing in every black land!. . .
> we have one weapon . . . the weapon of unity, of a marshaling of
> every anti-colonialist spirit and purpose . . . this dangling in our
> separate helplessnesses, this dancing attendance upon some met-
> ropolitan parties' inability to see eye to eye, these are the days of
> our weakness and of our defeat.[13]

Getting down to specifics, Césaire continued:

> This isn't the desire to go it alone, nor disdain for every alliance.
> This is the desire, the intention not to confuse alliance for subordina-
> tion . . . the peril stems from some of the very glaring deficiencies
> we notice in French Communist Party members: their inveterate
> assimilationism; their chauvinism . . . their as good as primary con-
> viction—which they share with the European bourgeois—of the
> omnifarious superiority of the West; their belief that evolution as
> it has come about in Europe is the only sort possible . . .[14]

This condescending attitude of "colonialist paternalism" for which Césaire coins the word "brotherlyism," as it specifically applies to the Communist superiority complex, deprives so-called "backward peoples" of the right to think for themselves:

> If the aim of all progressive politics is someday to restore their free-
> dom to colonial peoples, then the day by day activities of progressive
> parties must at least not contradict the supposed objective and not
> every day wreck the very bases, the organizational as well as the
> psychological bases, of this future freedom; and those bases boil
> down to one postulate: the right to take the initiative.[15]

After this unprecedented attack on the Soviet and French Communist Parties, Césaire concluded, almost naively,

---

[11]*Ibid.*, p. 8.
[12]*Ibid.*, p. 8.
[13]*Ibid.*, p. 9.
[14]*Ibid.*, pp. 9-10.
[15]*Ibid.*, p. 11.

. . . it's neither Marxism nor Communism I repudiate . . . what I want is that Marxism and Communism be harnessed into the service of colored peoples, and not colored peoples into the service of Marxism and Communism.[16]

Calling for a "Copernican revolution" in the habits and thinking of Europeans, he expressed hope in Chinese Communism, which his color-conscious soul was compelled to look upon favorably.

Turning to the specific case of Martinique, Césaire deduced "that the French Communist Party is utterly incapable of offering Martinique any prospect whatsoever that is not sheer utopian illusion."[17] Stating unequivocally what he had only implied in his other writing, Césaire accused the communists of having "managed to slip the hangman's noose of assimilation around our neck . . . isolate us in the Caribbean Basin . . . sunder us from Black Africa."[18] Then speaking of Africa, Césaire reasserted its primacy as a dynamic force for négritude, in contrast to the basic frame of reference of communism:

> . . . this Black Africa, the dam of our civilization and source of our culture, it's to her I look for the regeneration of the Antilles . . . Instead of that we are offered solidarity with the people of France; with the French proletariat and, via communism, with all the world's proletariats . . . There are no allies by divine right.[19]

Lapsing into philosophical abstractions, Césaire terminated his letter by noting:

> There are two paths to doom: by segregation, by walling yourself up in the particular; or by dilution, by thinning off into the emptinesses of the 'universal.'
> I have a different idea of a universal. It is of a universal rich with all that is particular, rich with all the particulars there are, the deepening of each particular, the coexistence of them all.[20]

This sensational letter has been excerpted at length not only for its obvious relevance to Césaire's political philosophy, but because its significance transcends any study of Césaire himself. It not only "ranks high in Pan-African literature and, one would hope, also in the wider political literature of our times,"[21] but it has been referred to as "one of the classical texts of anticolonialism."[22] Perhaps its most valid contribution, however, is its unequivocal illustration of the dichotomy between communism, as it has evolved, and the major predilections of the Negro world.

It has been said with regard to Soviet policy, if not practice, that

[16]*Ibid.*, p. 12.
[17]*Ibid.*, p. 14.
[18]*Ibid.*, p. 14.
[19]*Ibid.*, p. 15.
[20]*Ibid.*, p. 15.
[21]Colin Legum, *op cit.*, p. 106.
[22]*Le Monde,* September 11, 1962, p. 8, col. 3. (My translation.)

> Russia has an almost magic appeal among Negro peoples, not because
> the Negroes love democracy less than other people, but because they
> hate race prejudice more . . . They welcome the Soviet policy of
> racial equality, sometimes with an indiscriminating enthusiasm which
> causes them to overlook the evils of dictatorship.[23]

What Césaire's letter does is to dispel any illusions these Negro peoples may have had about the promise of International Communism for them.

"As a black, I never found precisely where I fit in,"[24] Césaire told this author in summing up his relationship with the Communist Party.

It seems reasonable to conclude, therefore, that, drawing on Césaire's experience, at least, Communism and négritude are fundamentally incompatible: of the two, négritude is by far the more vital force for the world's black people. In his public retort to Césaire's letter, Maurice Thorez revealed an awareness of the dynamics of the irreconcilable conflict. Railing against those opportunists who joined the Communist Party after victories against Hitler and who attacked the party from within (an obvious reference to Aimé Césaire), he concluded:

> It certainly seems that such men have not always made a sufficient
> effort to assimilate our principles, to understand the fundamental
> class principles of communist policy.[25]

Of course, what Thorez characterized as a lack of effort is more accurately the black man's unwillingness to subordinate his négritude to the basic tenets of communism. And, undeniably, the fact that Césaire denounced communism after a decade of first-hand experience and confrontation with it lends his arguments additional force and credibility in the black world.

---

[23] Paul Blanshard. *Democracy and Empire in the Caribbean*, p. 347.

[24] My interview.

[25] *Le Monde*, November 16, 1956, p. 5 col. 3. (My translation.)

VI
MATURITY — Expanding Visions

In his writing before 1956, Césaire was concerned mainly with the renaissance of the Negro heritage and the unmasking of colonialism. After 1956, there was a notable shift of emphasis: Césaire now concentrated on scrutinizing the problems of decolonization and independence for black countries.

If anything, after his resignation from the Communist Party, Césaire's intellectual approach to the general question of decolonization seemed to have become more extreme. At the Second Congress of Negro Writers and Artists in Rome, March, 1959, he delivered an impassioned discourse entitled "The Intellectual and His Responsibilities." Beginning with the announcement that colonialism was in its death throes, he continued,

> . . . decolonization is not automatic . . . decolonization is never the result of a voluntary decision of the colonizer's conscience. It is always the result of a struggle, always the result of pressure. Even the most peaceful of decolonizations is the result of a break. And I also say that all decolonizations are not of equal value. This is proved by the unequal development of liberated countries.[1]

Elaborating on these two points, Césaire sounded very much the ardent revolutionary:

> It is clear for us that there is not, there cannot be, bad *decolonization* in itself . . . the worst *decolonization* will always be a hundred fold superior to the best colonization. . . .
> . . . true decolonization is that which understands that its task is the complete breaking up of the colonial structures.
> . . . the struggle against colonialism is not terminated as soon as one thinks and *because imperialism has been militarily vanquished.*
> In short, our task is not one of shifting colonialism or interiorizing servitude. We must destroy it, annihilate it in the true sense of the word, that is to say rip it out by the roots, and that is why true decolonization will be revolutionary or not at all. This viewpoint enables one to understand how vain the attempts by certain people are to give credit to the idea that between the colonial epoch and the era of freedom, one must arrange stages and transitions.[2]

This passage is unequivocal enough; it asserts the cardinal revolutionary assumption that every vestige of present antipathetic institutions must be totally and immediately destroyed. This uncompromising position illustrates a certain dichotomy between Césaire's words and actions: for at the time he delivered this speech he was no less than a Deputy in the French National

---

[1] Aimé Césaire, "L'Homme de Culture et Ses Responsabilités," *Présence Africaine, Deuxième Congrès des Ecrivains et Artistes Noirs,* No. spécial, 26 mars-ler avril 1959, Tome I, p. 116. (My translation.)

[2] *Ibid.,* pp. 118-119.

Assembly, a liaison in the parliamentary apparatus between his 'oppressed' and 'enslaved' country and its colonizer. His words leave no room for such compromises to achieve goals, to participate in transitional periods or tactical alliances—the only possible justification for a true revolutionary's retaining a seat in a government he seeks to undermine.

The explanation for the revolutionary outburst in this speech lies perhaps in the nature of the audience which Césaire was addressing. Black intellectuals almost expected it of him, for his success in and his attraction for the black world was originally due to his aggressive new ideas and his impassioned total commitment to his cause, their cause. Perhaps he could not pass up the opportunity for an emotional offering that would appeal both to Negro intellectuals from newly independent nations and to colonial peoples for whom revolutionary ferment was a necessity for the struggle toward independence. And the delegates who listened enraptured to Césaire's speech did not seem disturbed by the seeming paradox of his status within the French Parliamentary system.

In 1961, as if to reappraise the basic assumptions of that very framework of French laws, Césaire wrote a unique historical study of the French Revolution in Haiti (Saint-Domingue), superimposed upon a biography of the island's Negro independence leader, Toussaint Louverture. In a short introduction, Césaire gave his reasons for having chosen the title subject:

> Haiti is the first country of modern times to have brought up as a practical issue and to have posed as a problem, and that in all its social, economic, and racial complexity, the great question that the twentieth century is trying desperately to solve: the colonial question.[3]

In the study that follows, he was very careful to delineate between the "French Revolution" *per se* and the revolution "du type colonial," which took place simultaneously. However, he draws a parallel in the rhythm of events which proceeded by means of Constitutionnels, Girondins, then Jacobins in France and whites, mulattoes, then Negroes in the colony. Césaire's differentiation between the aims and achievements of the Revolution in the metropolitan and in Haiti is founded on his incisive analysis of the plantation economy and racial situation which characterized the latter. In France, the emphasis of the Revolution was on the demand for equality of rights by the Third Estate (based on an economic phenomenon). In the colonies, however, there were three distinct problems: the definition of political ties between the metropole and the colonies, the arbitration of the declared conflict between mulattoes and whites, and "the most formidable of them and that which one scarcely dared to formulate, of the course to take on Negro slavery."[4]

[3] Aimé Césaire, *Toussaint Louverture*, (Paris: Présence Africaine, 1961.) pp. 21-22. (My translation.)
[4] *Ibid.*, p. 11.

For Césaire, the exigencies of anti-colonialism are defined by the correct response to these three problems which incorporate the double aspect of the colonial question—social and national. In his analysis of the revolutionary attitudes in these three areas, Césaire delineated his own conclusions.

Taking the national problem first, Césaire described it as a function of the economic problem, for the *raison d'être* of the colony was as a commercial extension of the metropole. It was, therefore, essential that only the metropole control the colony's affairs. This condition touched the very heart of the French bourgeoisie's interests, and according to Césaire, only one man of the Revolution correctly understood the situation and its alternatives. That man was Marat. Césaire quoted from an article written by Marat in 1791, in which he discussed the colonial demands for independence:

> The basis of all free government is that no people be subjected to the laws of another people, that they shall only have the laws given to them by themselves, that they are sovereign in their own land, and independent of all human power . . .
> *it is absurd and senseless that a people be governed* by laws which emanate from a legislator living 2000 *leagues away* . . . all have the right to free themselves from the metropolitan yoke, and to choose another sovereign, or to set up a Republic . . .[5]

For Césaire the important point here is the right of the colony to choose its own destiny and to administer its own affairs on an equal footing with the metropole, which may or may not lead to federation with the metropole as the best alternative for the colony.

This same equality of rights pertains to individuals and was the basis for demands for constitutional as well as well as political rights by the mulattoes. This group, analogous to the Third Estate in France, formed the middle class of the colonies. By virtue of this position, their interests prevented them from pushing the Revolution to its logical extreme—the solution to the Negro question.

It is this abomination with which Césaire was mainly concerned. Toussaint Louverture is the symbol of the liberation of the Negro slaves, the achievement of which represents the ultimate success of the revolution. It was on this point, the revolutionary potential of the Negro, that Césaire tried to reconcile his philosophy with Marxism. (Even after his break with the Communist Party, Césaire considers himself a Marxist.)

> Marx contrasted the worker to the peasant and spoke of the revolutionary vocation of the industrial proletariat massed in the huge centers as opposed to the sedentarism and conservatism of the peasant. One can see what European references explain such a concept. But as for the colonies? . . . Here, there is no property but lack of ownership in the absolute degree. Here there is no dispersion, but regroupment; no separation or scattering but on the contrary, concentration

---
[5]*Ibid.*, p. 175.

and cohesion. Marx praised the factory as the laboratory of the revolution. But is not the slave, more than the peasant, already a *rural proletarian,* and is not the 'colonial plantation' already a little like a factory?[6]

After having traced the revolution in the colonies to its logical conclusion, based on the foregoing evaluation of the Negro slave, Césaire surveys the results:

First result: the Negroes gained their liberty, and rose from the void. But also, for the first time, colored men, freed from a humiliating tutelage, no longer thought of themselves as a race, an oppressed race, but as a class, a conquering class.[7]

Thus, according to Césaire, the revolutionary class in the colonial countries is based unequivocally on race: the conquering class is the liberated Negro race; and the successes and failures of the Revolution are measured by the imperatives of the racial question.

But in spite of this obvious orientation along racial lines, as demonstrated by these conclusions, there is one extraordinary feature of *Toussaint Louverture* which moderates Césaire's "racism" and gives it some balance, at least. Here, for the first time, Césaire carefully and rationally differentiates between various white viewpoints in their attitudes toward Negro questions. His painstaking study of the statements of men involved in the French Revolution reveals a very sophisticated awareness of nuances of opinion, makes objective observations about prejudices and finally concludes that "during the Revolution two colonial policies confronted each other: the politics of principles and the politics of interests . . . in spite of some fortunate accidents, it is only too true that the politics of interests won out. . . ."[8] This would seem a rather mellowed Césaire, for whom there are now some grays where there had been only blacks and whites, and for whom the entire white world is not, by definition, racist.

In addition, this book offers incontrovertible proof of the profound debt which Césaire owes to his French heritage. He not only reveals his extraordinary understanding of the basic assumptions of modern French politics and culture, but also his acceptance of these principles as valid. In fact, he clearly does not question the validity of "Liberté, Égalité, Fraternité," but rather abhors the gulf between principle and reality in metropolitan-colony, white-black relationships. The problem is how to push men to implement the requirements of the principles they evoke, when those principles run counter to their own interests. In this regard, Toussaint, himself, represents for Césaire the liaison between the principle and its realization:

[6]*Ibid.,* p. 34.
[7]*Ibid.,* p. 214.
[8]*Ibid.,* p. 308.

The struggle of Toussaint-Louverture was the struggle for the transformation of a formal right into a real right, the struggle for the *recognition* of man and that is why he and the revolt of the Negro slaves of Haiti will go down in the history of universal civilization.[9]

In the last six years, Césaire has brought his négritude to bear on the current problems of the black world and the implications of its struggle for independence. He chose a trilogy of plays to illustrate the situation of the black man in the modern world:

> The black world is going through an extremely difficult phase. In particular, with the acquisition of independence by the African countries, we have entered into a time of responsibility. Blacks from now on must make their history. And the history of the blacks will truly be what they will make of it . . . a black writer can not enclose himself in an ivory tower. There are things which have to be understood . . . it is necessary to speak clearly, speak concisely, to get the message across—and it seems to me that the theater can lend itself to that, and it does lend itself to that very well.[10]

The first play, entitled *La Tragédie du Roi Christophe* (1963) deals with Haiti after the war of independence against France, when Henri Christophe had inherited the mantle of leadership from Toussaint Louverture and Dessalines. The second play, *Une Saison Au Congo* (1967) is the portrayal of Lumumba's short-lived career as leader of the newly independent Congo republic. Both plays are, therefore, concerned with the efforts of a Negro leader to forge a black nation out of a former colony: the inevitable problem is that of the chaos of decolonization and independence.

Haiti was the logical choice of background for the first of Césaire's trilogy—it was the first black country to gain its independence (1801), the first country where négritude proved itself; and Christophe represents the first black man faced with the necessity of building a State after independence has been gained. The alternatives are clear:

> Christophe: Either we destroy everything, or we redress everything . . . we must bear the burden: higher and higher. Further and further . . . We must go forward.[11]

But this is no easy task; rather it is perhaps more difficult than the gaining of independence. As Christophe puts it in the play:

> Haiti has less to fear from the French than from itself! The enemy of this people is their own indolence, impudence, hatred of discipline, propensity for pleasures and languor.[12]

Césaire's preoccupation with the people's lack of will to work for their new state of freedom indicates an evolution in his concept of universal equality,

---

[9]*Ibid.*, p. 310.

[10]Césaire, quoted in Magazine Littéraire, *op. cit.*, p. 30.

[11]Aimé Césaire, *La Tragédie du Roi Christophe*, (Paris: Présence Africaine, 1963,) p. 79. (My translation.)

[12]*Ibid.*, p. 30.

from emphasis on its acceptance in principle to concentration on the dynamics of its implementation.

> If there is one thing which irritates me as much as the remarks of the advocates of slavery, it is to hear our philanthropists clamor, with the best of intentions no doubt, that all men are men and there are neither whites nor blacks. This is unrealistic idle thinking . . . All men have the same rights. I subscribe to that. But within the common lot some have more duties than others. That is where there is inequality. An inequality of demands, do you understand?
>
> . . . .
>
> more is required of the Negroes than of the others: more work, more faith, more enthusiasm, a step, another step, still another step and keep what was gained at each step![13]

Thus, the requisite for independence and universal rights for Negroes is ultimately their own diligence. But leadership in this endeavor is of prime importance both to mobilize the masses and to assure the moral and cultural rearmament of the nation. It is these conclusions, drawn from Haiti's experience, which Césaire found most relevant for all incipient black nations.

The natural sequel to *Roi Christophe* was *Une Saison Au Congo,* the tragedy of Lumumba and a modern African nation in the birth pangs of independence. Within this framework, Césaire further evaluates the relationship of the leader to the people in an emerging nation. Lumumba personifies the revolutionary, the visionary, the poet-leader who lights the fire of Africa, the African conscience at its most intense moment." His greatness was to deny reality, his genius to conceive of a united Congo . . . to transcend reality."[14] And, in spite of his failure, Lumumba represents for Césaire an indispensable element in the blacks' fight to establish themselves: he alone inspired the latent national consciousness, he sowed the seeds for a future state. "The Congo can only be rebuilt," said Césaire, "by starting with Lumumba."[15]

Ultimately, Césaire's two dramas of hero-leaders leave unresolved the myriad problems endemic to decolonization and independence. Both Christophe and Lumumba fail, though for different reasons: Christophe, relentless and tyrannical, because he "would serve liberty by means of slavery!"[16] Lumumba. democratic, imaginative, religious, a victim of "the cold world of logic and interests,"[17] because he could not unify his country. What Césaire unremittingly underlines are the twin requisites of industry and inspiration for black nations' success.

---

[13]*Ibid.,* pp. 61-62.

[14]Aimé Césaire, "La Grandeur de Lumumba Etait de Nier La Réalité," *Jeune Afrique,* April 17, 1966. p. 29.

[15]*Le Monde,* October 7, 1967. Interview by Nicole Zand.

[16]Césaire, *La Tragédie du Roi Christophe, op. cit.,* p. 99. (My translation.)

[17]Césaire, *Une Saison Au Congo,* (Paris: Aux Editions Du Seuil, 1966.) Back jacket (My translation.)

In another vein, Césaire touches also on the vital forces at work in the relationships between these nations and the white world. Throughout these two plays, Césaire's perennial distrust of the white world is evident in his mocking disdain for its subservience to form, its skepticism toward the newly emerging nations, its detrimental contributions to the colonies, its eternal big-power maneuverings. But, he does not preclude the necessity for cooperation on the international level. In fact, he advocates it, but emphasizes that relations with the white world should be based on the principle of "la neutralité positive,"[18] a pointed reminder that a Negro nation has a unique heritage and should align itself neither with the Occident nor with the East.

Rounding out his trilogy is A Tempest (1969), an adaptation of Shakespeare's play, in which Césaire proposes to depict the situation of the black man in the United States. Prospero represents the conqueror, the man of reason who dominates and opposes Caliban, the man of instinct, of nature, the slave, the worker, the peasant, the Antillean. Ariel is the man of science, the intellectual, pressed into the service of power, in the person of Prospero. Faced with the domination of Prospero, Caliban and Ariel have two alternatives: violence (read, Black Panthers) and non-violence (read Martin Luther King and Malcolm X). Both are working toward the same goal: liberation.[19]

Significantly, "liberation" connotes something different in the American context than elsewhere. Speaking in a recent interview about his play and its relation to the American situation, Césaire commented that had there not been racial segregation in the United States, there would not be a black problem today, for it was segregation that preserved the uniqueness, solidarity and, therefore, the vitality of black culture. Furthermore, the two races are inextricably bound together, forced to live together, compelled to seek liberation through peaceful coexistence and the establishment of a love-hate—or hate-love relationship.[20]

---

[18]Ibid., p. 108.
[19]Césaire, quoted in Magazine Littéraire, op. cit., p. 37.
[20]Ibid.

VII
POLITICS — Accommodation and Adjustment

On the local Martinique scene, Césaire's popularity and influence are legendary. From 1945 to the present day, he has been re-elected Deputy to the National Assembly and Mayor of Fort-de-France in every election: a continuous record stretching over 27 years, surviving his unending philosophical peregrinations and the several changes in his political stance.

In 1951, the Communist Party, under his leadership, polled 62 percent of the vote.[1] After renouncing the Communist Party, in 1956, Césaire resigned his posts as deputy and mayor. At the same time, 18 other "conseillers," of whom sixteen were communists, also handed in their resignations.

A new election was called in 1958. Césaire returned to the polls as leader of his own independent party, Parti Progressiste de Martinique (PPM). Not only was he easily re-elected, but the list of candidates he endorsed amassed 82 percent of the vote; the Communist Party polled four percent.[2] The election confirmed Césaire as an independent politician with a considerable personal following.

Although he was one of the staunchest supporters of departmental status for Martinique in the 1946 referendum, the cornerstone of Césaire's political program since 1958 has been to reject that relationship for a very different one with the French Republic.

At his party's congress in 1958, Césaire declared:

> departmentalization removed power from the country, removed administration from the administered and increased centralization. And when too many things are decided in Paris, that amounts to saying most often that too many things are imposed by Paris. In other words, the system carries with it a risk of tyranny.[3]

Thirteen years later, Césaire is convinced that the "risk" has become a reality. "[Departmentalization] has proven to be a marvelous instrument of tyranny. The word is not too strong," he said recently. "The colonial regime had absolutely nothing over this one."[4]

Speaking of the current regime, Césaire declares that it is humiliating and anachronistic; oppression is inherent in France's extreme centralization; the Martiniquais have been made beggars; cultural assimilation has become self-destructive. In short, what he now considers the Martiniquais' naive search for equality has become a ruse of history.[5]

---

[1]*Le Monde,* January 1-2, 1956, p. 2, cols. 3-4.

[2]Sir Harold Mitchell, Bt. *op. cit.,* p. 97.

[3]Césaire, "Pour la Transformation de la Martinique en Région dans le Cadre D'Une Union Française Fédérée," report presented to the constitutional assembly of the Parti Progressiste Martiniquais, March 22, 1958. p. 5.

[4]Quoted in interview with *Le Nouvel Observateur,* March 1, 1971, p. 33.

[5]My interview.

50

As an alternative, Césaire advocates autonomy. Vague as to its immediate implementation, he envisions its first stage as "provisional" and "open," affording the Martinquais a chance to choose what "conforms to our interests."

There are, however, two principles which are fundamental to Césaire's notion of autonomy. First, Martinique would be assured continued self-determination by her own deliberative, decision-making legislature and responsible local executive. Secondly (and Césaire insists there is no inherent contradiction between the two), an autonomous Martinique must remain within the framework of a French federation.

Thus, while governing herself, Martinique would reserve "certain domains" for the central government—and by implication, certain obligations.

For very practical reasons, Césaire emphasizes that autonomy and independence are not synonymous, and he rejects the latter as vehemently as he embraces the former. He is keenly attuned to the fact that the average Martiniquais is terrified of independence and considers starvation the alternative to maintaining the *status quo.* Playing on such fears, the central government and its supporters on the island easily confuse Césaire's distinction between autonomy and independence, insinuating that the one makes the other inevitable.

On a more sophisticated level, official French reaction to Césaire's demand for autonomy is that nothing is possible between departmental status and total independence. And no one in Martinique has forgotten the lesson of Guinea, which defied Paris by choosing independence in 1958 and was unceremoniously cut off without a centime.

After touring overseas departments in 1971, M. Pierre Messmer, Minister of State for Overseas Departments and Territories, said:

> People have the right to demand autonomy, but they do not have the right to think that internal autonomy will permit them to continue on the basis of our national legislation. The fundamental option is between the departmental status and something else. But if a people wants to maintain its important advantages, they will have to maintain the departmental status.[6]

Césaire candidly thinks the implied ultimatum is a somewhat empty threat. In a recent interview with the author, he reviewed his current attitudes toward Martinique's relationship with France:

> While we cost France something, we also give her something in return. They don't just keep these departments for the fun of it. They have their strategic, sentimental, geopolitical reasons.[7]

---

[6]*Le Monde,* June 11, 1971, p. 11. My translation.

[7]My interview. All subsequent quotes of Césaire, either direct or indirect, are from my interview with him, unless otherwise noted.

He denounces French policy as ignoble blackmail, "forcing us to choose between our soul and our stomachs," and he despises French aid and security as "charity" and "paternalism."

> France could aid us indefinitely and never resolve our problems. I am partial to the Chinese proverb that it is better to teach a starving man how to fish than to give him a fish.

But Césaire in no way suggests that France stop sending Martinique the "fish." He clearly recognizes that having to go it alone completely would cause "economic terrorism." He is very much aware of the importance of the schools, roads, health facilities, housing, electricity, welfare, etc., which French funds provide. He also accepts the notion that the French presence is some guarantee in a "dangerous world."

"If we were asking for independence," he says, scrupulously maintaining his distinctions, "we'd have to look elsewhere for aid." But in a federal system such as exists in the United States, for example, Césaire reasons that the various states are self-governing in many ways and have their own budgets, and the federal government, in turn, makes grants to them or subsidizes special federal projects.

If such a relationship existed between France and Martinique, he argues, the island could continue to receive French funds. The method of distribution would be different, but local initiative and control of economic and political matters, both of which he considers mandatory, would be realized.

Although assuming, with a note of false modesty, that he would play "a certain considerable role"[8] in a new, autonomous Martiniquais government, Césaire is difficult to pin down with regard to a well-defined program he would institute. His campaign for autonomy, in fact, rests more on attacks on departmentalization than on coherent proposals he would support.

For example, Césaire has argued that as a department, Martinique is becoming progressively underdeveloped. Not only are the new industries not coming in, but old ones are being abandoned, as for example, sugar cane. It is a matter of "life and death" that the island industrialize, he says. Industrialization, in turn, depends on two things: protective tariffs and a program designed and funded specifically for that purpose.

But, laments Césaire, "the establishment of a customs barrier for the defense of local industries is incompatible with the departmental status." Furthermore, in spite of its special fund for the development of overseas

---

[8]Obviously, if Martinique ever voted for autonomy, Césaire would emerge as a national leader, since he is the architect and chief exponent of the idea. Some, who are skeptical about the whole notion, are also skeptical about Césaire's leadership. Gaeton Absalon, a successful Martiniquais businessman observed: "Twenty four hours after Martinique became autonomous, they would kill Césaire . . . when the cashier's window closed."

departments (FIDOM), the central government "has taken no initiative what-soever for the financing of an industrialization program for the island."[9]

Martiniquais industry, Césaire points out, should correspond to the resources and needs of the island. It should derive first and foremost from agriculture, with the aim being to develop a capability for the island to feed herself.

"Martinique is underdeveloped and it's true there is an exodus from the country to the city. The first thing for us to do is to put every Martiniquais to work . . . and we must start by making work in the countryside."

As a practical matter, he is aware that in spite of the stigma it carries and his past opposition, the sugar industry has to be revitalized within the economy—not to revert to a monoculture, but rather to establish a base for agricultural industrialization.

Throughout his discussion of the development of Martinique's economic capabilities, Césaire is never very far from a conscious or subconscious dependence on French funds. And, he always assumes they will be forthcom-ing, even if Martinique's needs run counter to France's interests. For example, a prime matter for reevaluation, according to Césaire, should also be the island's involvement in the Common Market. He is particularly irked that Martinique's Conseil General was not consulted by Paris before the island was committed to the Market. Gaining a captive market for Martiniquais sugar isn't necessarily worth the candle, Césaire feels, if it means "invasion" by Common Market products with which Martiniquais industry cannot hope to compete.

"It is shocking," exclaims Césaire, "that we have to eat beef from the metropole and import chickens from all over the Common Market, to say nothing of drinking all sorts of things when we should have juices made here from local fruits . . . if we were autonomous, we could at least decide for ourselves if we want to remain as part of the Common Market . . . after studying it objectively."

Césaire's evaluation of Martinique's relationship to the rest of the Caribbean is also vague, at best. The political makeup of the Caribbean is striking in its diversity, he observes. "Different traditions mark the islands, making it difficult for them to live together. They are self-centered and short-sighted," he adds, citing the abortive British Caribbean Federation of 1958.

For Martinique, he continues, a simple Caribbean identity would be too narrow, not taking into account the island's African heritage or French ties. He is, in fact, so geared toward Europe and Africa that he is unfamiliar with other Caribbean leaders.

---

[9]Césaire, "Pour la Transformation de la Martinique en Région dans le Cadre D'Une Union Franç-aise Fédérée," *op. cit.* p. 4.

"One has to be realistic," he says. "The Caribbean exists only as an ideal . . . a psychological reality, and maybe an economic reality, which is where one has to start . . . An autonomous Martinique will try and establish ties with our closest neighbors: Caribean and, especially, South American. It is necessary to reverse the artificial trends in our history."

It is in denouncing the cultural depersonalization and "loss of identity of a whole people" that Césaire mounts his most virulent attack on departmentalization. In this area Césaire, the poet, is most at home and most easily relates to his constituents.

He rankles at the humiliating administrative necessity to ask permission in Paris to build a school in Fort-de-France. But he is even more indignant about the curriculum imposed by the central power; newspapers and television controlled by the federal government; and fashions and art inspired by the capitol.

In contrast to the political and economic domains, however, Césaire and his PPM have sponsored a private school in Fort-de-France to provide an appropriate cultural and educational curriculum. The school, which now has about 250 students, who pay 50 FF per month, holds regular classes in the Creole dialect and offers French as a foreign language. In addition, Martiniquais history and geography, including technical geography, are taught along with Martiniquais literature.

The PPM also runs "Action Culturelle," a municipal school for dance, music, art, and eventually, theater, designed "to give back to Martiniquais folklore its purity and originality."[10]

In general, however, Césaire's is an emotional approach. He lacks any clearly articulated practical political or economic programs for Martinique. This seems evident in his long record as mayor of Fort-de-France. And, there is near-hysteria in his description of the city as a "municipal ghetto" in which his life, as the "opposition mayor" (to the Gaullists, whom the prefect represents), is made "very difficult."

"We are on the eve of 1789 . . ."[11] he was quoted as saying recently. In fact, there is no evidence to support such a view, and the majority of the population seems totally unaware of it.

Responsible observers attest to the fact that as a municipal administrator, he is totally inadequate. He allows whole systems, such as transportation, to wallow in disarray. Encouraging the poor to stream in from the countryside, he does nothing to prevent their becoming squatters, dependent on welfare, and contributing only votes for Césaire to the fabric of the city's life.

---

[10]This discussion about the PPM's schools was held with Césaire's Executive Secretary, Renaud DeGrandmaison, outside Césaire's office.

[11]Quoted in *Le Nouvel Observateur, op. cit.* p. 34.

"There is a lack of discipline, a *laisser-aller,* which is present in every aspect which is dependent upon the city," attested Gaeton Absalon, a mulatto businessman with 45 men working under him. "He plays politics instead of running the municipality."[12]

"Fort-de-France is the worst-run city in the Caribbean," argued Louis Lepouliquen, editor-in-chief of *France-Antilles,* the largest newpaper in the area. "Césaire has also never made a serious proposal on the floor of the National Assembly . . . Aimé Césaire, the statesman, is a myth!"[13]

Yet, almost everyone agrees that if Césaire is neither a statesman nor a great politician, his personal popularity among his constituents is undeniable.

From the political point of view, Césaire's stand on autonomy actually represents a minority opinion on the island today. The majority, who are content with departmental status and vote for the Gaullist party in national (French) elections, consider the PPM too radical. At the same time, the vociferous, but small, leftist ranks find Césaire's refusal to advocate complete independence from France proof of his too moderate bent.[14]

In Fort-de-France, however, where the level of political sophistication is the highest and there is the greatest cross-section of political attitudes, Césaire's following does not waver. In fact, in 1971, the last mayoral election, he polled 75% of the vote—9% more than in his 1965 victory.[15]

The people who steadfastly support Césaire adore him as the poet of négritude, even though they may never have read *Notebook on Returning Home.* They admire him for having declared his independence from the powerful Communist Party in 1956, though they may not fully understand his reasons for doing so.

Many of his constituents know of Césaire's moving testimony at the 1962 Marseilles trial of young Martiniquais radicals accused of threatening the nation by posting manifestos calling for "Martinique aux Martiniquais."[16]

---

[12] Gaeton Absalon, director of a printing company, Fort-de-France, Martinique. Quoted from my interview with him, August 1971.

[13] Louis Lepouliquen, Editor-in-Chief of *France-Antilles,* Fort-de-France, Martinique. Quoted from my interview with him in his office, August 1971.

[14] The Communist Party, which has become strongly anti-departmentalist, has also come to grips with the strong local feeling of antipathy for the idea of separatism, and it, too, advocates only a form of autonomy. The PPM and the CPM ostensibly have formed a kind of coalition for autonomy, but it is an uneasy alliance, at best, and any joint statement issued by them is a signal for separate interpretations, accusations and denials. Said Césaire of the alliance: "We have a tacit agreement — peaceful coexistence — to win autonomy for Martinique. But there is rivalry and competition, too. For example, we disagree on influencing the masses. On that question, it is either them or us: I want the masses to be a force, to be active. The Communist Party is not open and flexible . . . they are extremist in their methods."

[15] The figure was confirmed by almost everyone I talked to in Martinique, but there were some, for example, the Prefect, Jean Terrade, who bluntly declared that the elections had been fixed.

[16] *New York Times,* December 11, 1963, p. 9 col 3. Of the 18, five were convicted and got up to three years in prison; 13 were acquitted. The students were Martiniquais home for a summer vacation from their studies in France. They had formed the "Organization of Anti-Colonialist Youth of Martinique" (O.J.A.M.)

And Césaire is remembered as the one who spoke up to de Gaulle on his 1964 visit to Martinique and asked when the island would enjoy a role within the Republic comparable to that which the former African colonies were assuming.[17]

Malraux recognized Césaire's popular role when he toured the overseas departments to assure their affirmative vote in the 1958 referendum on adherence to the French Community. The outlook was bleak, he wrote, because the Antilleans might vote "no" to register their discontents. But what worried him most in Martinique was that Césaire, the key to the island, had not yet committed himself. When they appeared together before cheering crowds, Malraux was reassured.[18]

There is a certain mystical quality about Césaire's popularity. He has variously been called "the king of folklore," "the champion of the black race," "the greatest black poet of the French language," "the most prestigious politician in the Antilles," "a nonentity," and "a political failure."

But perhaps the current Prefect of Martinique, Jean Terrade (who would have no reason to praise Césaire), summed it up best: "Césaire is the symbol of the successful black . . . here, he is 'The Leader,' comparable to de Gaulle in this respect."[19]

On balance, it seems clear that Césaire must be regarded as a spiritual leader rather than as a statesman. Doubtless, he would agree. While in Fort-de-France (he spends a good deal of the year in Paris in his capacity as deputy to the National Assembly), Césaire goes every morning to his simply appointed office to dispose of his duties as mayor. Tropical rains and heat are kept out by fluttering venetian blinds. He sits at a desk littered with objects of Martiniquais folk art and daily receives dozens of what he terms 'the little people.'

"They come asking me for roads, schools—for everything—even things that aren't within my power," he told this author in his soft-spoken, extremely articulate manner. Then he added:

"That's to be expected. I am mayor. But obviously, they don't just consider me their mayor . . . they have a tendency to confuse me with another: God, the Father . . ."[20]

---

[17]There is an interesting account of De Gaulle's visit to Martinique in March, 1964, (*Le Monde*, March 24, 1965) in which it is related that the mobs in the streets went wild for the General who, raising his arms to the skies said, "My God, my God, how French you are!" In addressing him later, however, Césaire minced no words in pointing out Martinique's problems and in calling on France to help solve them, starting with the renovation of her institutions.

[18]André Malraux, *Anti-Memoirs*, trans. by Terence Kilmartin, (New York, 1968), p. 109. The Antilles voted 80% "yes" eventually. Of course, the incident also reveals Césaire's close ties with France, and even De Gaulle.

[19]Jean Terrade, Prefect of Martinique. Quote from my interview with him in his office in Fort-de-France, Martinique, August, 1971.

[20]My interview.

VIII
TODAY — Black Between Worlds

A roving reporter sent to Martinique in 1962 summed up what he called the "phénomène Césaire":

> Aimé Césaire has great powers of seduction. On first contact, his charm operates: his elocution, his empassioned look, his convincing gestures, right up to his political positions which his enemies call ironically his 'successive sincerities': anti-assimilationist at 25 years old, champion of departmentalization at 35 years, at 50 he has reverted to his former positions . . . In spite of these recantations, Aimé Césaire has remained a prophet in his country.[1]

His "sincérités successives" are clearly evident in the details of this study. But, surely, Césaire is no Machiavelli; rather, he is simply not a very practical politician. Even after many years in the role, he is an uncomfortable philosopher-poet in politician's clothing.

"I have tried to give a feeling of dignity to the people of Martinique," Césaire told the writer in a retrospective mood. "I wanted them to have a soul in the world . . . I haven't been able to realize very much. I was beaten in advance. I was swimming against the current."

However, just as he is almost incapable of expressing himself in hard political terms, the vagaries and ineffectiveness of his political postures should not be allowed to obscure the fundamental consistencies and far-reaching effects of Césaire's philosophical attitudes. The latter have proved more coherent and viable than any temporary stand he may have taken in their name.

The most self-evident, as well as the most compelling force for Césaire, is his black identity. It defines and shapes his philosophies, his art, his politics. It is the hallmark of his involvement with all black peoples in a common, worthwhile heritage and demands his commitment to struggle for their inalienable right to equality. It is this black identity that motivated, powered and sustains the "négritude" movement, first given literary expression in Césaire's *Notebook on Returning Home.* It was a sense of a worldwide black community that impelled Césaire home in the thirties and attracted him to the Communist Party. It was, paradoxically, the same black identity which prevented his ultimate surrender to Marxism and communism, concepts which require an overall view based on class, instead of race, and identification with the white proletariat of the world. It is also his black identification which aligns him with advocates of a "neutral third world," bound neither to the Western nor the Socialist bloc. Finally, it is his black identity which designates Césaire, a Martiniquais, one of the guiding lights of the Pan-African movement.

---

[1] *Le Monde,* September 11, 1962, p. 8, col 3. (My translation.)

The other element of continuity in Césaire's attitudes is the influence of his French cultural background.

Because of the very nature of négritude, critics of Césaire have often pointed out that these two elements constitute an insoluable contradiction. Some critics point to the paradox with exasperation:

"Aimé Césaire sings of négritude, but he is more European than African. He speaks of the dignity of black people in France, but he is the perfect example, the proof, of what a black can achieve in France."[2]

His attachment for France underlies still another irony, perhaps, for it may have precluded Césaire's ever becoming a really dynamic, revolutionary, black activist leader. There is evidence that Césaire experienced inner conflicts between his black identity and his French heritage. But the two are not mutually exclusive, and when all the dogmatic adornment is stripped away, what is left is that Césaire knows, and has in many ways come to terms with, his dual character.

The influence of Césaire's French cultural background manifests itself on three levels. The first has to do with his quality as an intellectual and poet: Césaire is considered by many, including himself, heir to the great French philosophers and poets. The second is demonstrated by the simple fact of his having been a Deputy in the French National Assembly for over 25 years. His commitment to the French parliamentary system is demonstrably stronger than any thoughts he may have had at one time about the violent revolutionary overthrow of the French government in Martinique. And by his own analysis, participation in the French National Assembly, by definition, precludes the demand for complete independence:

> . . . to accept being a member of the National Assembly, was to recognize oneself a member of the nation; to integrate oneself into the nation; to recognize the legislature of France as the valid legislature for the colonies and to render inconsistent in advance an eventual demand for independence.[3]

Finally, Césaire consistently affirms his unassailable belief in the humanistic principles inherent in his French heritage. Césaire's objective is solely

> To take literally the declaration of the rights of man . . . to show that there is no outcast race; that there is no marginal country; that there is no exceptional people . . . to embody and particularize a principle . . .[4]

---

[2] My interview with Lepouliquen.
[3] Césaire, *Toussaint Louverture, op. cit.*, p. 37. (My translation.)
[4] *Ibid.*, p. 310. (My translation.)

It is against the truths of "liberté, égalité, fraternité" that Césaire measures the quality of human relationships; if he is enraged with the whites of the world, it is because they have not universally applied their own exalted principles. And if he is occasionally impatient with the blacks, it is because they don't appreciate their responsibility in transforming the principle into a reality. Above all, Césaire knows it is *his* responsibility as a black intellectual to assert the equality of rights and, thereby, to restore the dignity of the black peoples of the world.

BIBLIOGRAPHY

I. BOOKS

Baldwin, James. *Nobody Knows My Name*. New York: Dell Publishing Company, 1961.

Balink, Albert. *My Paradise Is Hell*. New York: Vista Publishing Corporation, 1948.

Bernard, Jean. *Ces Îles de France - Guadeloupe et Martinique*. Paris: Editions de la Table Ronde, 1964.

Blanshard, Paul. *Democracy and Empire in the Caribbean*. New York: The Macmillan Company, 1947.

Coulthard, G.R., ed. *Caribbean Literature*. London: University of London Press Ltd., 1966.

_____. *Race and Colour in Caribbean Literature*. London: Oxford University Press, 1962.

Delaunay-Belleville, André. *Choses et Gens de la Martinique*. Paris: Nouvelles Editions Debresse, 1963.

Developments Towards Self-Government in the Caribbean. A Symposium held under the auspices of the Netherlands Universities Foundation for International Cooperation at The Hague, September, 1954. The Hague: W. Van Hoeve Ltd., 1955.

Fajon, Étienne. *La Lutte Pour La Paix en Algérie*. Discourse. Paris: Imprimerie Poissoniére, 1956.

Fermor, Patrick Leigh. *The Traveller's Tree*. New York: Harper & Bros., 1950.

Gratiant, Gilbert. *Île Fédérée Française de la Martinique*. Paris: Editions Louis Soulanges, 1961.

Guérin, Daniel. *Les Antilles Décolonisées*. Introduction by Aimé Césaire. Paris: Présence Africaine, 1956.

_____. *The West Indies and Their Future*. Translated by Austryn Wainhouse. London: Dobson Books Ltd., 1961.

Heyrel, J. *La Martinique et Son Avenir*. Paris: Les Éditions Françaises, 1957.

Juin, Hubert. *Aimé Césaire: Poète Noir*. Paris: Présence Africaine, 1956.

Kesteloot, Lilyan. *Aimé Césaire*. Paris: Éditions Pierre Seghers, 1962.

Legum, Colin. *Pan Africanism: A Short Political Guide*. 2d edition revised. New York: Frederick A. Praeger, Publishers, 1965.

Leiris, Michel. *Contacts de Civilisations en Martinique et en Guadeloupe*. Paris: UNESCO/Gallimard, 1955.

Malraux, André. *Anti-Memoirs*. New York: Holt, Rinehart Winston, 1968.

McCloy, Shelby T. *The Negro in the French West Indies*. Kentucky: University of Kentucky Press, 1966.

Mitchell, Sir Harold, Bt. *Europe in the Caribbean*. Stanford: Stanford University Press, 1963.

Murch, Arvin W. *Political Integration as an Alternative to Independence*. Ph.D. dissertation for Yale University Graduate School, 1967. Ann Arbor: University Microfilms, Inc. 1968.

Naipaul, V.S. *The Middle Passage*. New York: The MacMillan Company, 1963.

Nathan, Fernand, ed. *Aimé Césaire*. Paris: Fernand Nathan, Classiques du Monde, 1967.

Nettleford, Rex. *Mirror, Mirror: Identity, Race and Protest in Jamaica*. Jamaica: William Collins and Sangster, Ltd. 1970.

Parry, J.H. and Sherlock, P.M. *A Short History of the West Indies*. London: MacMillan and Co. Ltd., 1956.

Piquion, René. *Négritude*. Port-Au-Prince, Haiti: Imprimerie de l'Etat, 1961.

Poole, Bernard L. *The Caribbean Commission*. Columbia: University of South Carolina Press, 1951.

Pouquet, Jean. *Les Antilles Françaises*. Paris: Presses Universitaires de France, 1952.

Revert, Eugene. *La Martinique*. Paris: Nouvelles Editions Latines, 1949.

Sable, Victor. *La Transformation des Îles d'Amérique en Départements Français*. Paris: Larose, 1955.

Senghor, Léopold Sédar. *On African Socialism*. New York: Praeger Paperbacks, 1964.

Wilgus, A. Curtis, ed. *The Caribbean: British, Dutch, French, United States*. Gainesville: University of Florida Press, 1958.

II. PERIODICALS AND NEWSPAPERS

"Aimé Césaire." *Jeune Afrique*. (April 17, 1966), 28-29.

"Aimé Césaire." *Le Nouvel Observateur*. (March 1, 1971), 33-35.

Alba, Victor. "Communism and Nationalism in Latin America." *Problems of Communism*, VII, No. 5 (September-October 1958), 24-31.

Alonzo, Manuel de Moya. "Communism in the Caribbean." *Vital Speeches*, XXIII (September 15, 1957), 712-16.

Beloux, François. "Un Poète Politique: Aimé Césaire." *Magazine Littéraire*, No. 34 (November, 1969), 27-32.

Blanshard, Paul. "Twilight of Caribbean Imperialism." *Nation*, CLXVIII, No. 4 (January 22, 1949), 92-94.

Bondy, François. "French Intellectuals Say No." *Partisan Review* (Winter 1957), 86-94.

Caribbean Studies. Institute of Caribbean Studies. University of Puerto Rico, *passim*.

Desanti, Dominique. "La Tragedie du Roi Christophe." *Jeune Afrique*, No. 161 (December 9-15, 1963), 26.

Fanon, Frantz. "Antillais et Africains." *Esprit* (February 1955), 261-269.

Geismar, Peter. "The Wretched of Martinique." *The Nation* (June 23, 1969), 782-783.

Gosset, Renée and Pierre. "Martinique: Unspoilt Beauty of the West Indies." *Réalities*, No. 42 (May 1954), 52-61.

Jahn, Janheinz. "Aimé Césaire." *Black Orpheus* (1958), 32-36.

Kiejman, Claude. "Martinique et Guadeloupe: Départements Français ou Terre Etrangères?" *Le Monde Diplomatique*. (October 1971), 16-18.

Koshland, Miriam G. "The Literature of the French West Indies." *Books Abroad*, 30 (Summer 1956), 275-277.

"La Francitude de la Martinique." *L'Express*. (August 3-9, 1970), 54-55.

Le Monde. 1956-1972. (As cited in footnotes.)

"Martinique" an Interview with Aimé Césaire. *L'Express*. (May 24-30, 1971), 80-81.

New York Times. 1959-1972. (As cited in footnotes.)

Présence Africaine, Le 1er Congrès International des Ecrivains et Artistes Noirs. No. spécial. September 19-22, 1956, Paris.

Présence Africaine, Deuxième Congrès des Ecrivains et Artistes Noirs. No. spécial. March 26-April 1, 1959, Tome I. Rome; Paris.

Rivlin, Benjamin. "De Gaulle's French Community." *Current History,* 36-37. (May 1959), 278-283.

Robinson, Kenneth. "Alternatives to Independence." *Political Studies,* IV, No. 3 (October 1956), 225-249.

"The End of Empire, Another View." *International Affairs,* Vol. 30 (1954), 186-195.

Time: Special Issue "Black America 1970". (April 6, 1970).

Williams, Eric. "Contemporary Patterns of Race Relations in the Caribbean." *Phylon,* XVI, No. 4 (December 1955), 367-379.

III. WORKS BY AIMÉ CÉSAIRE

"Appel à la Population." Fort-de-France: Imprimerie Bezaudin, 1957. (Election article).

"L'Appel au Magicien — Quelques Mots Pour Une Civilisation Antillaise." *Martinique,* No. 1 (1944), 16-17 (Magazine article).

Les Armes Miraculeuses. 2d edition. Paris: Gallimard, 1946. (Anthology of poetry, includes play "Et Les Chiens Se Taisaient").

Cahier D'Un Retour Au Pays Natal. 2d edition. Paris: Présence Africaine, 1956. (Poem).

"Crise Dans Les Départements D'Outre-Mer Ou Crise de la Départementalisation?" *Le Monde,* Paris, March 29, 1961, p. 5, cols. 1-2. (Newspaper article).

"Culture et Colonisation." *Présence Africaine, Le 1er Congrès International des Ecrivains et Artistes Noirs.* No. spécial. September 19-22, 1956.

Discours Prononcé à la Sorbonne en Commémoration du Centenaire de la Revolution de 1848 – April 27, 1948. Paris: Presses Universitaires de France (1948), 20-33. (Speech).

Discours Sur Le Colonialisme. 3rd edition, revised and augmented. Paris: Présence Africaine, 1955. (Monograph).

"L'Homme de Culture et Ses Responsabilités." *Présence Africaine, Deuxième Congrès des Ecrivains et Artistes Noirs.* No. spécial, March 26-April 1, 1959. Tome I.

Letter to Maurice Thorez. Paris: Présence Africaine, 1957. (Letter).

"Pour la Transformation de la Martinique en Région dans le Cadre D'Une Union Française Fédérée." March 22, 1958. (Rapport présenté au Congrès Constitutif du Parti Progressiste Martiniquais). (Political speech).

Parti Progressiste Martiniquais. Pamphlets, campaign literature, announcements: many are written by Aimé Césaire.

Une Saison Au Congo. Paris: Editions du Seuil, 1966. (Play).

Le Soleil Cou-Coupé. Paris: K Editeur, 1948. (Anthology of Poems).

Toussaint Louverture. Edition: revised, corrected, and augmented. Paris: Présence Africaine, 1961. (Historical study, subtitled "La Révolution Française et Le Problème Colonial").

La Tragédie du Roi Christophe. Paris: Présence Africaine, 1963. (Play).

IV.   PERSONAL INTERVIEWS: all conducted by the writer in Fort-de-France, Martinique, August 1971.

Aimé Césaire, Mayor of Fort-de-France, Deputy to the National Assembly. Two interviews, on successive days in his office.

Jean Terrade, Prefect of Martinique.

Pierre Furstein, Managing Editor, *France Antilles*.

Louis Lepouliquen, Editor-in-Chief, *France Antilles*.

M. Ernoult, Director, Department of Agriculture, Martinique.

Gaeton Absalon, Director, S.I.G.A., Fort-de-France.

M. Don Don, architect, Fort-de-France.

Renaud De Grandmaison, Executive Secretary to Césaire.

Informal conversations were also held with people representative of the general population: hotel workers, taxi drivers, shopkeepers, women in the markets, etc.

V. GOVERNMENT PUBLICATIONS

VIe Plan de Développement Economique et Social (1971-1975), No. 1371. Paris, 1971.

"Martinique," 1970 Statistical Reports, Départements D'Outre-Mer. Paris.

Institut D'Emission des Départements d'Outre-Mer. Rapport D'Activité, Exercice 1969. Paris, 1970.

Index